A Scoop Of Honey

ASHLEY HETHERINGTON

ISBN-13: 978-1-0907-4763-1

TABLE OF CONTENTS

ACKNOWLEDGMENTS

Thank you is such an understatement. Thank you Nancy Wells, Lisa Kuhn, Lauren Tesi, Layne Jones, Caroline Atlas, Brooke Waid, and Maddie Huels for giving me feedback and helping me make this book the best it can be (and make sure I don't include anything stupid.)

Alyssa Brooks - you are sent from heaven above. Thank you for all your help with the design and marketing work for this book. This would not happen without you. Thank you for encouraging me when I really didn't want to continue, and always helping me get on my own two feet when I've fallen down hard. You are a gift.

Mom and dad - thank you for always believing in this dream to write a book. You two never gave up on me and my unconventional career plans. I would not follow them unless I had you believing in me, and I feel so blessed to have you on my side. Mom, thanks for making me coffee and more coffee while I woke up early to write this book. You have never stopped believing in me. Dad, thank you for making me laugh and introducing me to the power of words. If it weren't for you, I'm not sure I would've developed such a love for the written word. Thank you for editing this book and providing your editing wisdom. You've never stopped cheering me on. I can't wait for the challenge of our next crossword puzzle.

Thank you to my brother, Will, for believing in me as well. I'm so happy we finally became friends when we grew up.

Thank you to my people. Greek Gathering, The LAKE, "Let's not", Cherry Poppins (yes, this is my house name). Our little community has changed my college experience for the better, and you all have shown me what true friendship looks like. Thank you for all of your support with this book.

Thank you for all those of you who read *The Honey Scoop* in your free time. You have made me fall in love with writing and the impact it can make on people.

Thank you to Crossroads Church for being a home away from home for me. I don't know where I'd be without you.

And most importantly, thank you Jesus, for giving me a story I could write about, and for showing me who I really am. What a gift that is.

INTRODUCTION

For years, I thought Christians were so weird. And that they never had any fun, or never laughed at genuinely funny things, so I tried my best to avoid them.

But my perspective on faith eventually changed, because I found that most of the places I was looking for fulfillment just weren't working for me. I had a long run of searching for my purpose in different places, all of which left me feeling like there was something more out there.

I went on my own faith journey without the help of anybody. I didn't have anyone to talk to about all my questions without feeling embarrassed. I only wished I had a resource at the beginning of my faith journey that would help me get started.

My hope is to be the resource for you that I never had. I want to be a mentor for you and be here for your questions about God and faith and this whole Jesus-thing. My hope is to provide the information as you're exploring your own questions.

This is a book for people who are dipping their toes into the water of faith, but don't really know where or how to start.

We are going to cover all the Sunday school basics, for the gals that never went to Sunday school. I am not a pastor or a Sunday school teacher, and I certainly don't have a theology degree. I am a college girl who loves to write and has a passion for gals like us who want to learn more about what faith can look like.

This book is really just about what God has taught me over the years, and how to start a relationship with him. This relationship isn't a step-by-step thing, it's a beautiful process that only God can reveal to you. I am just a vessel to help you get there, and letting God do the real work.

Whether you are just checking this faith-thing out, or you want to know the next steps of friendship with Jesus, this book is for you.

So let's start this journey together, no matter where you're at or how much you know. Surely, He will take you to a better place than you could ever even imagine.

For more, follow along online!
Instagram: @thehoneyscoop
Email: thehoneyscoop@gmail.com
www.thehoneyscoop.com

HOW I ENDED UP GOOGLING JESUS

I was in 5th grade when I got held back in religious education.

I shouldn't have been surprised - considering I begged my parents to let me skip the weekly classes, and when my parents did manage to get me there, I dozed off and thought about the cute boy sitting next to me. I didn't know anything about Jesus or God or Moses, or whoever they talk about in religious education, nor did I care to know. So I was a bit clueless when it came to engaging in class discussion.

Every time the teacher asked a question, I tried not to make eye contact with her so she wouldn't call on me. This seemed to work, until one day, when it didn't. She was describing a biblical story, and she managed to lock eyes with me like a hawk eyeing her prey.

"Ashley, who did this?", my teacher said, asking about the main character in the Biblical story.

My face got really hot, while all the smarter, wiser Catholic 5th graders turned to look at me. I didn't listen to a word she said. My stomach turned to knots, and I didn't say anything for what felt like 5 minutes.

"Uhhhhhhh. I think it was....uhh...Jesus? Was it Jesus?" I responded.

She looked at me with disappointment. "No, Ashley. This was not Jesus."

I thought that was ridiculous. This was Jesus class, for crying out loud. How could Jesus not be the right answer for any one of these questions?

The next year I found myself sitting in a dusty classroom with all the other held-back Catholic misfits, one of which was my brother. Our family was represented quite well in the church, if you can imagine, between this and the fact that we only went twice a year.

The held-back class included reading an "Accepting Jesus" book with childlike illustrations on every page, and watching Biblical stories in claymation. Daydreaming about my latest crush got me through the hour.

Maybe it's from this experience, but it's safe to say that religion looked more like something I had to do than something I actually wanted to do. I checked out of the God-business pretty quickly, and moved on with my life.

Growing Up

My parents were both very kind people, and they treated me with nothing but love. My mom and dad taught me to respect others and showed me how to work hard. But I did not grow up in a home where we prayed before every meal or read children's books about the Bible.

My family would go to Christmas and Easter services, but every so often they'd want to go to a regular service. When I was forced to go to church, I would focus on staring at the architecture of the building and the intricacies of the murals. Gazing at the building helped me kill some time.

I didn't know any of the prayers, so I mouthed the word "watermelon" over and over again. Every Sunday, I couldn't wait to be done with church because there were free donuts after most services, the ones with the sprinkles on top. That may have been my ultimate motivation for going.

Nothing against the church, but it didn't exactly excite my 5th grade self, so donuts and architecture were enough to get me through.

Instead of finding my purpose in the walls of a church, I was out looking for it in how people saw me.

My Perceived Purpose

I learned at a very young age that I wasn't good enough.

I was in 7th grade when I found out my boyfriend and my best friend started dating behind my back. My relationship with him mainly included texting across our ENV3 flip phones, and making out at ice-skating rinks, but I really did like him. I had lost my boyfriend and best friend at the same time, which was devastating for a middle schooler. Instead of seeing this as an immature middle school relationship, I saw myself as the problem.

It wasn't the relationship ending that hurt me. It was how I *saw* the relationship ending that did the damage. This event told me that I did not quite measure up.

So when 8th grade came around, I was paranoid that the whole school and my friend group hated me. If these two people left me, surely they would too.

I started feeling anxious every time I talked to people, because I was so paranoid that they didn't like me. I felt so insecure that every time I was in a conversation with someone all I thought about was what they were thinking about me. The only people I felt confident to be myself around were my parents because I knew they were stuck with me.

I let the word "rejected" stamp my identity.

Because I kept to myself, my friends started distancing themselves from me, maybe because my insecurities were causing me to distance myself from everybody. I wouldn't be invited to sleepovers and I got excluded from a lot of things. I felt so insecure that my mom went behind my back to email all the other moms and tell them to invite me to things. This was mortifying, to say the least.

I don't want to put down these people - and who knows if I was even a good friend to them. But getting excluded from sleepovers and group chats communicated to my middle school self that I was not good enough. And if my close friends didn't like me, what did that mean for me? This is when I started to get depressed, and the braces, acne, and being in middle school certainly didn't help.

One day, I thought that the reason I was so low and sad and hopeless was because I *let* myself get to this point. I figured that I was the problem. I blamed letting my guard down and being vulnerable with the very same people that left me. And from that moment on, I swore I would never do that again.

And with that, the old Ashley was gone. The new one was here.

Because I felt like a friendless loser, I used acting to get me out of it. That's right, acting. If I couldn't feel confident, then I would just have to *act* confident, and then maybe I would feel better about myself.

I had a "fake it till' you make it" mentality. With this new character, this new me, my goal was to be more:

- Confident
- Funny
- "Queen B"
- Independent
- Sassy
- Bitchy
- Perfect

I felt if I put these traits on, like an outfit in the morning, then I would finally be enough.

I also saw this tactic as my protection from people hurting me. If I was acting as "new Ashley", then I couldn't get hurt if people didn't like me because I wasn't really being myself.

Here's an excerpt from my journal in sophomore year of high school: *I was shy, timid, and boring Ash. And now I'm onto sassy, independent, and brave Ashley Hetherington.*

Yep. This really does sound straight from a bad teen drama. And this new version of myself absolutely sucked. I don't know why I thought this was a good idea, but we do weird things when we get hurt.

I developed an intimidating, no-one-screws-with-me mentality. I never let people see me sweat because vulnerability to me equaled death. I would not be knocked off my feet again, and this is just how I did that.

I wanted to be noticed. So when I got my braces off and discovered self-tanner, as well as a bombshell bra, I found that I was finally getting noticed by guys. It boosted my confidence to hear other guys tell me I was beautiful, and how they saw me became a huge sense of my worth. They gave me the attention I was looking for.

I was mean. I started drama. I was selfish. All because I thought that if I wasn't, the world would eat me alive.

So here we are. Mess goes to mess.

I liked acting because it made me feel strong. All because I was scared of ending up alone, friendless and rejected, and I was terrified that would happen again.

And this acting was finally catching up to me. This is my diary entry from January 7th, 2014, just a couple months from the last one:

Lately, I haven't been feeling all sure of myself like I used to. It's funny, but the person I was acting like at the beginning of the year was so confident and had a bajillion guys talking to her. Now it's like I'm a completely different girl. All I know is the reason why I was acting like someone I wasn't was because I was afraid to be myself. I was afraid of hurting and letting people hurt me. Now I just don't know who to be.

I thought acting like you had it all together was the key to living a fulfilling life. I tried out classy, I tried out bitchy, snobby, smart. None of them left me with peace, none of them gave me the identity I was looking for.

I was an insecure mess. But God did not give up on me.

Imitation is Suicide

I remember one day I was in history class and I heard this quote that knocked me off my feet.

The quote said, "Imitation is suicide." (Ralph Waldo Emerson)

I looked at that and felt personally offended. But deep down, I knew it was true.

By acting like this other person, I was actually killing the real version of myself, digging her grave and ridding of her existence.

Hearing this blew me off my feet and led me to some truth I couldn't ignore anymore. I also couldn't keep fighting the emptiness I was feeling underneath the smile I put on every day.

With each guy I was with, with each mean comment I uttered, with each moment of conformity, I felt the tug. The gut feeling that I, Ashley, was completely faking it. And I really wasn't the girl I had tried so hard to be. I couldn't change myself to be more of what I thought people wanted me to be.

It became more difficult for me to fake a personality. It was becoming more exhausting. When you do something that isn't natural for months, it can catch up to you.

And me faking it still didn't stop people from rejecting me, which was the goal all along. My BFFs left my 16th birthday party to smoke pot. The guys I hooked up with told me they didn't like me back. And teachers gave me bad grades because they didn't think I was a good kid.

This idea that putting on a mask would get others to like me was not true. I couldn't make everyone happy, I couldn't be one hundred different people wrapped into one. It was all so exhausting.

Although I had crafted this image, there was still a part of me that never changed, something deep down to my core. I wanted to listen to music I thought was good, even if it wasn't popular. I wanted to be nice to people, instead of acting mean. I wanted to study hard and actually ask questions in class, instead of acting like a dumb girl with no ambition. I wanted a guy to treat me with respect, instead of spending time with guys who really didn't care about me.

But I didn't know how to be myself. I didn't know how to let go of the fear of disapproval. And most importantly, I didn't know how to experience true, complete freedom. Freedom from insecurity, freedom from people-pleasing, freedom from this confined space I had trapped myself in.

I distinctly remember a day when I was at an all-end. I sat on my couch in my living room and thought - "Who the heck am I?" I knew this girl I was trying to be was a fraud, and I wanted to know who I really was. I wanted to know what my purpose in life was. And most importantly, I wanted to experience real confidence to be who I was created to be, and to live without the fear of how others saw me.

I just didn't know how to get there.

It was then that I scrolled on Instagram and saw this girl who always seemed so comfortable in her skin. I admired the heck out of this girl because it seemed like she didn't really care about what others thought about her, and she was unapologetically herself. She also was so happy and confident all the time, but in a genuine way, and I wanted to be more like that.

I don't remember the exact caption of her picture, but it said something about Jesus.

My curiosity stepped in, and it led me to search Jesus on Google. If Jesus could give this girl the confidence that she has, then maybe this Jesus thing could give it to me too.

I didn't think this Google search would be a defining moment in my life. I thought it would be like everything else I tried - like all the pretending, all the striving, all the people-pleasing. But this was different.

And yet, the search led me to a weird website with italic words about accepting Jesus into your heart, and I found it a bit creepy. It reminded me of my church days where I felt bored and ready for service to be over. And if this Jesus thing was like that, then I wanted nothing to do with it.

I put my phone away and went on with my day.

The Book

A couple of days later, my best friend, Kelsey, came over to my house. We were sitting on my back porch talking about our day when she told me she needed to leave for book club. I asked her what book she was reading, and she said, "It's a book about finding your purpose."

Of course, my eyes lit up at the sound of that. I wanted to find my purpose so badly, so this was perfect timing. I was so desperate I would've probably joined a cult. Thankfully I didn't, but you never know how things could've turned out.

Kelsey told me she would buy the book for me, and that was that.

When she dropped it off, I was all excited. The cover read *The Purpose Driven Life* by Rick Warren. I was so ready to find my purpose, it was scary. This was the moment I had been waiting for.

I had expected the book to be all about me, and yet the subject came as a big surprise. Instead of the focus being about me, it was all about this guy named Jesus.

The author, Rick Warren, talked about people pleasing, which I had never heard of before. When I came across this part of the book, I knew he was speaking directly to my situation.

He said: "If you are looking to any human being to either make you happy or keep you happy, you are going to be disappointed eventually. Only God can meet all your needs. No person has the ability to give you all the security, approval, acceptance, and love you need regardless of what they promise you." (Rick Warren, *The Purpose Driven Life*)

It was like this guy was speaking exactly to what I was going through. He directed me to something different than I've ever tried before. He said instead of focusing on pleasing that person, focus on Jesus, who accepts you just as you are.

This news changed my life. I got the permission to be myself, to come as I am, which I had never gotten before from anything or anybody else.

I couldn't believe that I was created for an actual purpose, and that there was someone behind it. I couldn't believe there was someone out there who wanted me to be *me*. And lastly, I couldn't believe there was someone who told me I really was good enough, without needing to change.

I reread that book twice, I kid you not. This was just the best news for me. And when I started my days focusing on how Jesus saw me and trying to live for an audience of One, I started becoming more of myself.

CS Lewis said this: "Look for yourself and you will find loneliness and despair. But look for Christ and you will find Him and everything else." *(CS Lewis, Mere Christianity)*

For the first time in my life, I felt rejuvenated, my spirit hopeful, my soul refreshed. I was told that God had knit me together for a purpose, that he made every part of me with intent, and I would be doing a disservice to the world by hiding who I truly was. He was the ultimate stamp of approval I was looking for all along.

When people told me I was:
- Not cool enough
- Too annoying
- Too boring
- Didn't party enough

Jesus was telling me:
- Ashley is loved
- She is kind
- She is courageous
- She is my daughter

The more I looked to Jesus for my identity, the more I became myself. Since he created me, it only made sense for me to look to him for my worth, and my true self would shine through.

Here's a diary entry from this new time in my life.

January 1, 2016

For a long time, God, I have tried to be someone I'm not. I think you want me to realize I don't even have to try to be anything. My identity is created in you. I should get lost in you, instead of getting lost in trying to be "myself". I'm the person you've always wanted me to be.

I thought putting on different identities would fulfill me, and then I would be good enough. It was only until I found my identity in Christ that I actually felt whole and complete.

I say this as someone who once rolled their eyes at church-stuff, who thought the whole thing was a bunch of humbug. I say this as someone who was held back in learning about Jesus, which I think is funny to this day. I say this as someone who finally got the approval of others, but then ended up feeling like an empty shell of a human.

No wonder I was so unhappy, always searching, never quite satisfied.

But finally, all the things I was looking for, I had found. Not in myself, not in approval, not in something I did. But I found it in a person.

A person who gave me worth, purpose, security. A person who didn't ask for me to be perfect, who would stick by me no matter how many friends I had, and who actually had a plan for my life.

And what kills me is that there are some people who were just like old Ashley, who have no idea that this is out there. And that's exactly what led me to write this book.

A Relationship, Not a Religion

I learned through this experience that Jesus is not a religion. Jesus is a relationship. He is literal love, and when he comes into your life, he changes it and the way you see yourself, way more than any "religion" can.

I don't know if my story resonates with you. But what I do know is that we all have one. Some come in the form of an abusive relationship, an eating disorder, an unexpected tragedy. None of us live a perfect life and has seen everything go smoothly.

And I don't know why you picked up this book, but maybe you're like me and feel like you've tried just about everything to fix it, but something is missing.

My relationship with God was the missing puzzle piece of my life. Before I knew God, I was a hot mess. I was selfish and greedy, always striving for attention. But God stepped in and took me out of that mess I was in. He made my life about serving Him and loving others, instead of serving myself.

My goal from then on was not to imitate people I admired, or imitate this cool, sassy, confident person I wanted to be. It was to imitate Jesus.

For the first time ever, I found my self-worth in something that couldn't be taken away. Not with rejection, or disapproval, or even how I saw myself. I didn't look to likes, popularity, or even a guy to tell me I was enough.

Instead, I started to find my worth in someone whose opinion of me would never change, someone who finally told me I was enough. This was the very thing that set me free.

WHO IS JESUS, ANYWAY?

I ask "why?" to just about everything. It's one of my great quirks. So at the beginning of my faith journey, I had a ton of questions about who Jesus is, or if God and Jesus were the same thing, because nobody really addresses this concept at first. People just expect you to know the difference, even though it is largely complicated to someone who wasn't raised in a Christian home.

I also had a question about where dinosaurs fit into God's story - and this question was only partly answered.

And though I had a million questions, the fear of embarrassment kept me from asking anyone anything. I also didn't really know whom to ask, because I was such a newbie to faith in the first place, and didn't have any trusted counselors to talk to.

So from personal experience, I can only imagine what questions you have conjured up about this whole Jesus thing. I mean, this is all so new to you - so if you knew everything, I'd be a tad concerned.

That's why I thought of some questions that beginner Christians have, and answered them accordingly. Also, keep an open mind with the big concepts described here. They might sound crazy, like how on earth could we believe someone came back from the dead. But God is really cool, and creative, and if we were able to make sense of him, he wouldn't be God.

These concepts will take time to sink in, like grace and death and the Holy Spirit, so give yourself time to let these avenues resonate with you. They still are resonating with me today, and I *still* don't fully understand everything. Give yourself the space to not fully grasp everything at this point in your journey.

To dig into our faith, I think it's important to understand the story of my man JC, aka, Jesus Christ. I give most all my besties nicknames, and he is no exception.

To describe JC, we first have to talk about God.

His Name is Love

At the beginning of the world, like the OG beginning, there was God. He created everything that there is. The planets, the skies, the stars, and cute lil animals. He created everything you see around you, like the coffee from the Starbucks you drank this morning, and the beautiful beach you wish you were drinking it on. He made everything that is in existence today.

And even though he created all of these wonderful things, he still found that something was missing. And that something is you.

He knitted together both you and me in our mothers' tummies all for his love. With the creation of us, he finally had someone he could lavish with his love.

But he knew it wouldn't be real love if we didn't have a choice in the matter. We're not his puppets or his robots, where he's forcing us to love him back, like a narcissistic dictator.

He wanted a genuine and real relationship with us, and that would mean it would be a 2-way street. And for that reason, he gave us free will- the ability to choose whether we wanted to love Him back.

There was a time when our relationship with God was flawless. There was no beef, baggage or tension. We'll call this the "honeymoon phase". It was also called the Garden of Eden, with the creation of the first man and woman, Adam and Eve. Check out more of this story in the book of Genesis (you can read in your Bible or just Google it).

The Uh-oh Moment

In the iconic words of Hannah Montana, "Nobody's perfect". And that's where the problem began.

With the free will that God gave us, we chose, well, not God.

This is also what the Bible calls "sin". I know, sin is a scary word that doesn't make you feel warm and fuzzy feelings. We can just describe it as separation from God, because that is just exactly what sin is.

Because of the fall, humans are in a pickle. In this decision to turn away from God and choose our own ways, this resulted in an imperfect relationship with God. He stayed perfect, but we were left broken, and in a broken world, where our bond with him was not the same as it once was.

It's not a surprise that the world is broken. Our loved ones die suddenly. Our friends leave us. Our boyfriends cheat on us. Our relatives get cancer. Our parents get divorced. These are just a few of the many hard things that are a result of separation from God. We can see that it was not supposed to be this way, and it pained God so very deeply to see His beloved children struggling.

And in all of this brokenness, in all of this hurt - there has always been something in us that this world cannot fulfill.

God is love, but also just. For any mistake that's made, there's a consequence. And for separation from God- for this sin thing we're talking about- the consequence is death. Unfortunately, when we choose to go against God, we also choose the consequence that comes along with it.

God did not want death to be the end of our story. Even though, according to justice, we deserved it, He wanted to make a way for us to be saved from the consequences of our imperfections.

This is all super dark and scary stuff. But stay tuned- just like any good love story, there's a rescue plan in the making.

The Rescue Plan

Have you ever seen one of those action movies, where the hero jumps in front of a speeding bullet to save the one he loves? It's always an epic scene, where the audience is in awe of the sacrifice.

This is quite a good depiction of what JC did for us.

"For God so loved the world that he gave his one and only Son, that whoever believes in him shall not perish but have eternal life." (John 3:16 NIV)

To rescue us, God took on the form of a man, who went by the name Jesus. He was born 2000 years ago in a manger. and walked the Earth. He laughed at jokes. He slept probably around 8 hours a night. He probably used some hip ancient Hebrew slang with His friends. And yes, he even pooped.

Jesus performed miracles. He preached about forgiving your enemies, and thought that everyone, even the lowest of society, should be treated with love. He washed the feet of people, he was kind, he was different. He gave the world the best example of what it looks like to love one another. And this excited some people, and alarmed others.

Because he is God, and God is perfect, Jesus never made a single mistake in His entire life. He never sinned, nor did he fall short of perfection. And because he didn't sin, not even once, He was the only person who wasn't worthy of death. He is the only person who ever walked the Earth and lived a perfect life, so He would have been the only one eligible to escape death.

But yet, he chose to die so we wouldn't have to bear the weight of our mistakes, and so we would be made right with God once and for all.

When I was growing up, at my church, I would stare at this statue of Jesus hanging on a cross. This would kind of freak me out, and also confuse me, because I had no idea why he was up there in front of everyone. Seeing him hang on that cross looked incredibly painful. I just didn't understand any of it. I had no idea why people would encourage that.

But JC died on the cross for a distinct reason, and that reason was for us. This was the ultimate sacrifice for every mistake that's ever been made. He took on the weight of the world's mistakes- jumped in front of the speeding bullet for who He loved- so that we could live. He took on the form of a sinner and received the punishment we deserved so that we could be looked at as blameless in the eyes of God. He took our place.

Getting crucified is the worst way to die. It is long, gory, and humiliating. It was miserable for Jesus to be up there for hours in excruciating pain- especially since He didn't deserve it. And because he is God, he could have definitely gotten down from the cross and avoided the pain if He wanted to.

But nope. He chose to stay up there and do what needed to be done to make our relationship with Him right again. He did this all for us, because that is just how much he loves us. The Bible says "But God demonstrates his own love for us in this: While we were still sinners, Christ died for us" (Romans 5:8 NIV). If that's not the most beautiful rescue story you've ever heard, I don't know what is. You aren't just listening to this love story for other people, but you are a part of it as well.

Because we were imperfect and affected by sin, we actually were the ones that deserved to die on the cross, not Jesus. We deserved this penalty because the "wages of sin is death" (Romans 6:23 NIV).

But because Jesus is so loving, he died the death so we wouldn't have to. He made it easy for us to experience life and forgiveness, and all we have to do is believe in him. And most importantly, he provided access to a perfect relationship with the God of the universe.

We deserved to die for our mistakes, because they are, well, ours. But Jesus broke this system. He took the bullet for us.

This is where Jesus is our hero. Because he lived a perfect life, one without sin, his death meant saving all of us with him.

When he died for us humans, we got a clean slate, no matter where we've been or what we've done. He died for any past, present, and future mistakes.

He came to mend our relationship with God - to give us life, not only eternal life but a fulfilling life on earth. Because of Jesus, we get to experience life and life to the full.

And that isn't even the best part.

Three days after getting crucified - JC rose from the dead. And death officially died. He beat death so we could live forever with Him.

When Christ died for us, our old selves died with him. This means any label we put on ourselves was done away with. The stamp of rejection had no hold over me anymore the minute I accepted Him into my life.

This means that when you accept Jesus, that label you've been under for so long is done away with. Maybe that label looks like abandoned. Not enough. Too much. Too annoying. Too fat. Too far gone.

Jesus takes every single one of those labels and throws them into the fire. He makes it so you are not a slave to those identities, and you can actually start over, this time in Someone who loves you and created you for a purpose.

When he rose, we rose with him, in the new creation he wants us to be. We now have a perfect Spirit in us, telling us who we are, instead of what we told ourselves before. We are not a slave to whatever we once were. Instead, we are free in Christ.

When you accept him, you are free to live in the identity he gives you - to be a child of God.

He did this all for us so we can experience his presence on earth, so we can talk with Him and have him actually answer, to walk with Him wherever we go, to have hope at the many different rock bottoms of life.

So you've heard of the Father, "God". You've heard of his Son, Jesus. But there is a third person, and that is the Holy Spirit.

The Spirit is Jesus' presence on earth. Because Jesus rose from the dead, He now lives with us on Earth through the Holy Spirit. God the father is on His throne in heaven, Jesus is advocating for those who believed in Him and accepted the sacrifice He made for them, and the Spirit is the presence of Jesus on Earth. This spirit has many gifts, being Jesus and all. And we will get into this in a later chapter. But once we accept Christ, his Spirit is not only with us, but *in* us forever. We have Divine power in us 24/7.

What is Grace?

After sin entered the world, following the rules was very important. The rules are also known for "the law". The law looks like running on a treadmill at full speed and never getting a break. It's a life of striving and never making a mistake.

The law tells us that we need to do everything perfectly, that we need to get everything right - which is very different from something Jesus shows us: grace. Grace tells us that we are cherished and loved by God, and there's nothing we can do to lose this love. It is lavished on us freely.

The law demands, but grace supplies. We can look at our day and only see the demands of all we need to do. Or, we can see that Jesus has already given us everything we need to get through the day through his Holy Spirit, and through his supply of grace. We need to work out the divine power he has given us.

"By his divine power, God has given us everything we need for living a godly life. We have received all of this by coming to know him, the one who called us to himself by means of his marvelous glory and excellence." (2 Peter 1:3 NLT)

If you want to know how this whole Jesus-thing can impact you, here's an example from day-to-day life.

You may have a huge exam to study for. Or maybe you have someone in your life who is really hard to love. Or, maybe you struggle to get out of bed in the morning because of the loneliness you feel. The law says, get yourself off your butt, you're on your own. Strive, strive, strive.

But grace says, look to Jesus, and he will strengthen you to get you through it. Because Jesus is in you, because there is a perfect Spirit in you, there is nothing you can't do that he would call you to do. Jesus is the one who gives you the motivation to study for an awful chemistry test. Jesus is the one who can forgive the person who hurt you. Jesus is the one who can strengthen you and give you hope for your future. Jesus may be the only reason you can get out of bed. But you will, my friend, because nothing is impossible for anyone who is in Christ.

The New Order

Remember that thing called free will? It still exists. Except this time, you don't need to be perfect. Loving God back does not mean being perfect and never making a mistake. Instead, loving Him back means one thing: accepting his son, Jesus, the one who came down to earth so you could live life to the full.

Accepting his love is a free gift. There are no terms and conditions. There is no test you need to take. There's no price you have to pay in return. And no, you won't get held back, like I did. Instead, you just need to receive it.

Let Jesus take all the baggage you carry, all the stress in your life. Let him take all the hurt in your life, all the tears. Let him take your shame that's built up from a horrible mistake you made years ago, but can't forgive yourself for. Let him take your broken heart. Let him take your insecurities, depression, anxiety. Let him take it all. These are the exact things he died for.

"Are you tired? Worn out? Burned out on religion? Come to me. Get away with me and you'll recover your life. I'll show you how to take a real rest. Walk with me and work with me—watch how I do it. Learn the unforced rhythms of grace. I won't lay anything heavy or ill-fitting on you. Keep company with me and you'll learn to live freely and lightly." (Matthew 11:29-30 MSG)

Allow yourself to release everything to Jesus. He isn't surprised by any of it.

Then, accept the joy he wants to give you on Earth, accept the wonderful plan he has for you, accept the friend that he wants to be to you. Accept His walk with you, no matter just how smooth or bumpy that walk is.

And once you let this love into your life, you'll never be the same. And that's for certain.

Accepting Love

If you read this story and you want to have a relationship with my man JC, I am so darn excited for you.

Accepting Jesus is very simple. You can do this with a close friend, or someone who has encouraged you in your faith journey. You can also do this with a parent or family member. You don't even need to do this with anyone, either, you can just be by yourself, in the comfort of this book. The only two people really needed for this are you and Jesus.

If you're ready, let's walk through the steps below to the next big chapter of your life.

Admit:

Firstly, admit that you fall short, and that you are imperfect. Admit that you are sinful, meaning you fall short of perfection.

Believe:

Second is to believe that Jesus is the Son of God, who lived a perfect life on earth and died on the cross for your sin so you could have a perfect relationship with God. You accept that he loves you enough to die for you so you can experience life to the full.

Tell God:

And lastly, tell God what you believe. The Bible says that anyone who believes with their heart and confesses with their tongue that Jesus is Lord will be saved.

So if you're ready to receive this wonderful gift of life, say this prayer out loud with me below:

"Jesus, I know that I've fallen short of perfection. I need you in my life, and I can't do this life without you. I believe you are the Son of God who died on the cross for my sins and shortcomings. I know you are the way to a fulfilling life. I am ready to receive your love. I trust you with my life, and I invite you to be Lord and Savior over my life. Let's live this life together. In your name, Amen."

Yup - it's that simple.

Now, Jesus is with you every day, all the time, 24/7. You now have direct access to God, forever and ever. He will make himself known to you with time, through his Holy Spirit. We will go over more of strengthening your relationship with Jesus in the following chapters of this book, but the first step is acceptance.

Should I Get Baptized?

Baptism is a wonderful way to express an inward reality of an outward declaration of faith. If you just prayed the prayer in the last chapter, I encourage you to get baptized at a local church to show your close friends and family the decision you've made with your life. You might want to do this on your own, if you don't have anyone to share this faith experience with. But it is super special to have your close friends together for such a special moment of your life.

Friend, it's only going to get better from here. From now on, you'll never be the same. The Bible says that you are now a new creation - "Therefore, if anyone is in Christ, the new creation has come: The old has gone, the new is here!" (2 Corinthians 5:17 NIV)

It's time to turn the page of the next big chapter of your life. Welcome to this new life - welcome to this new chapter. Time to turn the next page and see the beauty waiting for you, the light that is shining the very path you walk. What a beautiful, hopeful light it is.

Scriptures to Look To:

- "In the beginning was the Word, and the Word was with God, and the Word was God. He was with God in the beginning. Through him all things were made; without him nothing was made that has been made. In him was life, and that life was the light of all mankind. The light shines in the darkness, and the darkness has not overcome it." (John 1:1 NIV)
- "for all have sinned and fall short of the glory of God, and all are justified freely by his grace through the redemption that came by Christ Jesus." (Romans 3:23-24 NIV)
- "For God so loved the world that he gave his one and only Son, that whoever believes in him shall not perish but have eternal life." (John 3:16 NIV)
- "And surely I am with you always, to the very end of the age." (Matthew 28:20 NIV)

- "We love because he first loved us." (1 John 4:19 NIV)

Application

If you want to learn more about Jesus's story, I'd encourage you to head to the book of Matthew. This book tells the entire story of Jesus and is my favorite perspective of his story. Reading the words of Jesus will help him become real for you.

Also, after reading this chapter, write down some questions that you still may have. Then, if you have a trusted spiritual counselor, I encourage you to ask this person that question. Don't be afraid to ask out of the fear of embarrassment. It's important that we open up the floor to any and all questions, because this is how we learn. And lastly, the best source you could go to is God. Ask him to show up for your question and to answer it. He always shows up in the best way.

HOW DO I TALK TO GOD?

When people told me I could talk to God, I got a bit confused. How on earth could I do that? I didn't believe that he could actually hear me, because surely he had a lot of things on his to-do list, being the God of the universe and all.

I thought it was something like Santa Claus, no way he actually cared enough about what I specifically wanted for Christmas because he had the rest of the world to take requests from.

Since I grew up in a traditional church, I figured it was all "hallowed be Thy name" kind of stuff. And of course, I had no idea what "hallowed be Thy name" actually meant, so there's that.

But I learned that prayer is not as formal as you'd think. If you can talk to people, you can surely talk to God.

Talking to God is a lot like talking to a friend

In journalism class, I was told to talk about news like I was telling my mom. This helps you focus less on saying things perfectly and more on just getting the point across.

This method looks a lot like talking to God. We can tell the news of our lives to God, just like we are opening up to our mothers, or a best friend.

And you don't have to clean yourself up to do this, or even use complete sentences. You can actually be your weird, authentic self.

Think about it, God already knows who you are and what you are thinking. He even knows the funny sayings you revert to like "the point is" or "ya know?", so He wants you to use them with Him too.

He doesn't want to talk to the person you're trying to be. Instead he wants to talk to the real you.

This would be like if you and your best friend were super close, but then every time you started talking about something deep, you started saying weird formal things that totally break the vibe of your conversation. Eventually, she is going to tell that you are faking it, and then it's just going to be weird for everyone involved.

Also, talking to God like how we actually talk in real life is a lot more enjoyable. I don't know about you, but acting formal is not a very good way to develop a true relationship. Acting formal puts up a wall of perfection, and perfection keeps you from true connection.

Perfection keeps you from true connection.

Prayer is talking to God about anything and everything.

If this means bringing something that gave me a sour feeling in my stomach to him, then I will do just that. But if that means talking to him about a cute boy I saw in class, I will do that as well. Nothing is off limits, especially cute-boy-talk.

If something is ever making me upset, He wants to be the person that I vent to. And if something excites me, He wants to be in on that too, celebrating with me.

I tell him exactly how I am feeling. If I am feeling upset, I tell him about it. If I feel anxious, I tell him why. If I deeply don't like someone, I tell him how annoying I think this person is, and really hope that God agrees with me, but he rarely does.

This is why God and I are so tight. He loves me even when I am so brutally honest. Sometimes I laugh at myself when talking to Him because some of the things I say are flat out ridiculous.

I am certainly not a potty mouth. But when I am really, really angry, and I bring that to God, I may or may not let a few bad words slip. Please don't judge me.

But again, if he wants to be my friend, and he wants to build a relationship with me, what better way to hold up my end of the relationship than to come as I am - instead of trying to be someone I am not.

It's not about what you say or saying things perfectly. It's about believing that there is actually someone Divine listening to you, and that this Divine being is on your side. It's about trusting that you're not alone, and sharing your baggage with someone who can carry it.

God is not surprised by what we say. Instead, he's more alarmed when you don't talk to him about what is taking over most of your thoughts because he knows your thoughts already. The Bible even says "You know my thoughts before I think them." (Psalm 139: 2 NCV)

He came down to earth to have a relationship with you, to be your friend. Just like any relationship, the more you reveal, the closer you get.

This is a gift for anyone who feels they are in a place where they don't know how to trust, and they don't have anyone to really confide in. He can always be that friend for you.

What prayer looks like for me

Recently, I'm going through a big season of change- a storm, if you will. My boyfriend and I of 3 and a half years broke up a couple months ago. I thought that was just a little rain in my life, but little did I know the hail/sleet/monsoon that would be right around the corner. Like they say, when it rains, it pours.

After the breakup, my grandma died, my family went through this huge change, and my brother transferred from the college I go to. All of which sounds like a bad movie that no one wants to see.

At first, I did not handle all of this well. I was a big ball of 170 emotions, all swirling around in the same body, trying to get a word out. You can just imagine how frustrated I was, because I was a sprinkle of what-the-heck-is-going-on, a dash of anxiety, with a big cherry of insomnia on top.

Here is what my conversation looked like with Jesus the other night:

Scream yelling quietly so my parents don't hear me downstairs and get concerned

God, I am SOOOOOOOOOOOOOOOOOOOO pissed off. UGH. I just want to hit something!!!!

Why would you let this all happen at once? I am so angry. I just hate that all of this is happening.

What the &#%!@!!!!!!!!!!

God, I am not strong enough for this. I feel like a failure, this is not what I planned. And you know I love everything to go exactly as planned. I just don't know what to do.

Please help me. I just need help. You know how best to help me. In your name, Amen.

And that was that. Sounds a little concerning right? It's definitely does not resemble any "hallowed be thy name" prayer that you'd hear in Catholic mass. But I don't care. And neither does our God.

Not that this traditional prayer is bad - but I think there is something beautiful about bringing all our baggage to God in our own language, like he is our only friend to turn to in the midst of a life crisis.

When God responds to your prayer

You might be skeptical about that prayer, maybe I was a little too honest and a little too uncensored.

But the next night, after I prayed that prayer, I watched the first episode of *This Is Us*. If you haven't seen this show, please, for the sake of all humanity, turn it on after you finish this chapter. You have my permission.

In the episode I was watching, the main characters lose their baby to a miscarriage. A doctor comes by to encourage him, and he says these words:

"There's no lemon so sour that you can't make something resembling lemonade."

As I watched this scene, tears welled up in my eyes. God had answered me with something I needed to hear. No matter how sour life can get, there's nothing so awful that God can't make beautiful. And yes, He did answer my prayer through a sappy TV show, which makes me love Him even more.

I needed to be reminded that this pain will not be wasted, and it may be used for something better than I could even imagine.

It reminded me of one of my favorite Bible verses, "And we know that in all things God works for the good of those who love him, who have been called according to his purpose." (Romans 8:28 NIV)

And if that's not enough, I was driving home the next day from my friend's house, when I couldn't help but notice this huge, beautiful moon in the sky. This moon looked so close to the ground that if you were in a plane, you could reach out and touch it.

Oddly enough, the moon looked like an eye. Not all of the moon was showing, but only a portion, that was in the shape of a left-lens of a pair of sunglasses.

When I noticed this, a faint voice interrupted my moment. I heard,

"With my loving eye on you."

I got confused because I didn't know what that meant. It kind of came out of nowhere.

When I got home, I recognized "with my loving eye on you" from a passage of Scripture. Scripture is another word for a quote in the Bible. And if a line from the Bible pops into your head, then you know without a doubt that it's from God. The Lord put this specific line in my mind so I would go home and look it up.

When I found it, the full scripture read:

"I will instruct you and teach you in the way you should go, I will counsel you *with my loving eye on you.*" (Psalm 32:8)

After reading this verse, a wave of peace washed over me. I knew, in this moment, that God had literally seen me. I wasn't some tiny ant that he looked at from his throne, wondering how their life is going. Instead, he saw me, and he knew what was going on in my life. I felt seen, which is one of the most wonderful feelings when you've hit rock bottom.

I love to know the plan, make the agenda, and stick with it. So when life doesn't go as planned, and I can't make sense of anything, I will immediately go into panic mode. I figure if I'm not in control of the plane that is my life, then the plane is going down real quick.

But God knew my fears, my weaknesses, and he provided the encouragement I needed. He showed me that He has a plan, that He is in control, even though I felt like the plane of my life was about to crash into a nearby cliff. He gave me another moment of affirmation that everything is going to be okay, which finally let me breathe again. I could hope again.

You might think I am crazy for talking to God this way, but I know God is okay with it. I know that because *He responds.*

No matter how loud we yell at Him, no matter how imperfect we feel, no matter what mistakes we've made, no matter how many tears are streaming down our cheeks in one big ugly cry - He isn't phased.

Even in the raw and real moments of our lives, he responds, and he loves us despite any imperfections we have. Surprisingly enough, God didn't send His son to save the perfect people, with flawless tempers and unchipped nails and eloquent speech. Jesus says "It's not the healthy who need a doctor, but the sick" (Luke 5:31 NIV).

How open can I be with God?

I used to believe that I needed to go to confession to "confess" my sins. I remember one week during my religious education days, my dad told me it was time to go to my first confession. And with that, anxiety rolled in my stomach, and I immediately started thinking of all the bad things I'd done in my life that I needed forgiveness for.

I was trying to pick which "sin" I needed to confess, and this means that as a 5th grader, I guess I had a lot of sins to choose from. I debated between the sin of lying to my art class about having a horse named PB&J, or being mean to my little brother, which was quite a frequent occurrence.

Yet, with all this overthinking, I never even went to confession. Another reason I was probably held back.

My outlook on "confession" was filled with shame and fear like I needed to hide something or be punched in the gut for it. But bringing our crap to God looks a lot less scary than we would think.

We don't need to be afraid to bring things to God. He loves us so darn much, and he already knows our shortcomings, so we don't need to be sweating our butts off as we tell him whatever is in our hearts. We can bring our shame and guilt to him and he will not condemn us, but encourage us to choose the right thing next time. After we give Him all of our messiness in complete surrender, He wipes our slate clean and tells us to live in our true potential, the best version of ourselves, the person he has created us to be.

This reminds me of the prostitute who was dragged out to Jesus by some guys who asked if they should do something about her sins. They thought God was judgmental, wrathful, and eager to throw that wrath on the first person who made one mistake. But Jesus's response shows us that God is certainly not that way.

"They made her stand before the group and said to Jesus, "Teacher, this woman was caught in the act of adultery. In the Law, Moses commanded us to stone such women. Now, what do you say?" They were using this question as a trap, in order to have a basis for accusing him.

But Jesus bent down and started to write on the ground with his finger. When they kept on questioning him, he straightened up and said to them, "Let any one of you who is without sin be the first to throw a stone at her." Again he stooped down and wrote on the ground.

At this, those who heard began to go away one at a time, the older ones first, until only Jesus was left, with the woman still standing there. Jesus straightened up and asked her, "Woman, where are they? Has no one condemned you?"

"No one, sir," she said.

"Then neither do I condemn you," Jesus declared. "Go now and leave your life of sin." (John 8: 3-11 NIV)

When we mess up, God wants us to come to him instead of hide in our shame. Jesus doesn't condemn us for our mistakes. He isn't eager to punish us, but rather he is eager to take the burdens of those mistakes from us and make us new. This looks a lot like the word repentance, when we turn away from what's causing our shame and turn towards Jesus and accept his grace.

Listening For God

Listening for God is a lot easier than we might think. We can be grounded with these three things to go to when we want to hear from God.

1. Prayer

The first is prayer. When we bring our thoughts to God, and we trust them with him, we are also providing a space to hear from him.

And when we are facing a prayer that isn't quite being answered, we can always ask for wisdom on the subject and what God wants us to know. The Bible says, "If any of you lacks wisdom, you should ask God, who gives generously to all without finding fault, and it will be given to you." (James 1:5 NIV)

God promises that if we ask for wisdom or guidance, he will give it to us. This might be some of the best news for us incompetent humans. The God of the Universe, who know everything in all of existence, gives us access to this same knowledge. This trumps Google search any day.

And it's also great news for someone who wants to ask eight million people about the same thing before making a decision. Aka, that person is me.

2. The Bible

Another way to hear from God is to read the Bible. This book has incredible wisdom on whatever situation you are going through. Hearing His voice through the Bible might look like flipping through pages and seeing what jumps out at you and grabs your attention. Or it can look like reading stories and seeing what resonates with you. We will get more into digging into the Bible in a later chapter, but it's easier and certainly more fun than you'd think. It can actually change your life.

3. Community

The last way to hear from God is through a community. The Bible says, "For where two or three gather in my name, there am I with them" (Matthew 18:20 NIV).

We can bring what we are going through to like-minded friends, ones who want to help you discern where God is leading you. When you get in a space where you are with other Christians, you are much closer to hearing what God is trying to communicate to you.

And I know what you might be thinking, how terrifying it can be to step out of your comfort zone and look for some Christian community. I find in these spaces we can feel like we are not good enough to approach someone who seems way ahead of us, or who may even reject us.

I'll discuss community in another chapter, but when you move past fear and reach out to someone who is a strong Christian to be friends, the effort goes a long way. Also, you got nothing to lose. Going out of your comfort zone gives you so much opportunity to grow. Like a famous quote says, "What if I fall? Well, darling, what if you fly?" (e.h).

I will say that God is personal, and he wants to speak with you in a unique way. He may point to TV shows to speak to me, but he will show you just how he wants to get to you. It can take a while to get to this point however, so the best place to start is with these three different ways.

Make sure that no matter what, you pay attention.

If we are constantly on our phones, listening to music, and distracting ourselves - we are making it harder for God to reach us. God can't speak to you if He doesn't have space to.

It's the worst to be with someone who only talks about themselves. They yap, like a tiny dog in Petland, about everything going on with their lives, families, and even private information - the whole nine yards. And then while you are spending an hour and a half just listening and nodding, with your brain about to explode, they totally forget to ask you one single thing. Nobody likes to be in this position.

Talking to God can look a lot like this. Just like any relationship, if you talk the whole time, that isn't much of a relationship. There needs to be reciprocation, which involves listening just as much as you speak.

After you talk to him about something, you can close your eyes and try to hear what he is saying to you. This does not mean God is going to pop up in your room on a cloud and tell you exactly what to do with your problems. Although, this would be nice, and I wish it worked this way.

Hearing from Him involves asking him to talk to you, closing your eyes, clearing out the noise in your head, and giving Him the space to speak.

Application

I've reflected over my prayer process, but I want you to experience this divine communication, too. It will change your life.

If you can today, go into your room or in a quiet place, where it's just you and God.

And then tell Him what's going on. Tell him what's in your heart. Just like if a friend was in the room, asking you how you're really doing, talk to God like you would this friend.

I say my prayers out loud because I am an external processor. But you may want to pray inside your head. Whatever you prefer, it's up to you, there are no rules to this shindig.

Spill your heart out. If things are going great, praise him for that. If you need wisdom, ask him for answers. If you need to know he's listening, ask him to show up for you.

Be honest, be open. Tell him what's going on. And then ask him for what you need.

And then, listen.

Half of prayer is talking to him. The other is resting in his presence, listening for a word, or a direction. So when you pray, make sure to make room for a response. You'll be amazed at what you hear.

CHURCH 101

I used to absolutely dread going to church. It was like a workout, where I knew I needed to go, but I absolutely hated getting my butt there.

I always zoned out during the services and couldn't seem to keep still. To keep myself from going crazy, I would take regular trips to the bathroom to make the time go faster, which would include washing my hands for a really long time.

When I first got into my faith, I heard people talking about going to church, and actually being excited to go. I thought it was a bit weird, because it they were talking about the church that I knew, there was no way that was enjoyable.

But these Christians never made it sound boring, instead it was something they looked forward to every week. It was described as a space to learn, listen to good music, and meet kind people.

It was not until I walked into my first church home that I knew what people were talking about. The music was actually catchy and dance-worthy, and I actually found myself understanding and resonating with what the pastor was saying. And even better, I didn't get so bored to the point where I would need to take long bathroom breaks. This was a whole new world for me, and I liked it.

Every week after church, I felt this wonderful sense of peace. I walked out with an actual excitement, because I was learning more and more, and I was finding a place to call home. The messages were so good that I started to write down key points in my notebook, and then apply them to my week. I also made it a tradition to get myself a Tim Horton's iced cappuccino after service, which could have largely contributed to my peace as well.

Enjoying church wasn't something I had ever experienced before - but it felt good and right. Church became less of an obligation, and finally something I looked forward to every week. I knew that no matter what went wrong that week, church would always be a place for me to feel loved, and like I belonged. Little did I know this is what Jesus intended for us to have in our church all along.

You might have no idea what church to join, and that's completely okay. As someone who is really bad at making decisions, I completely get this struggle. Though I'd like to tell you otherwise, there is no "perfect" church for everyone. Unfortunately, there is no Buzzfeed quiz to tell you where to go to church. Churches vary, and you've got to walk through the doors to experience a service to see whether you feel at home.

The Beauty Of Church

Freshman year of college was a lonesome year for me. I didn't really have a church that I was going to, but I decided to check out this welcoming church called Crossroads.

(Warning: this is when you may feel bad for me. I feel bad for me in this too.)

They had a space where you could do your homework. It was finals week, and I had heard about this place having late hours for studying. And because I didn't have very many Christian friends, and finals are stressful, I figured this would be the perfect place for me to go. It was around 9pm, and I figured that this space would be open. Their space was off-campus, and since poor-old freshmen can't bring cars, it was up to me to walk there.

So you bet your booty I walked 30 minutes to this church-homework-space. It was cold and sad out, and I was definitely afraid of a murderer coming to get me from the bushes.

After 30 minutes of walking, I walked up to the front door of the building. I was alarmed to see that none of the lights were on. This was not a good sign.

I touched the doorknob and turned it, but it wouldn't open. Yep. I about cried my eyes out.

There was no one I could call to pick me up, so I definitely walked back in the dark, scary night for nothing.

Or at least that's what I thought.

I was bitter. I was having a bad semester and felt really lonely. I just wanted to feel loved and find a community of believers, and I thought I could get that at church.

I got over myself and went to the same place, now during the daytime. I went to sit down and do my homework. I looked around, and saw there weren't many people there that I could make friends with in this space. I was heavy-hearted.

All of a sudden, a guy walked up to me, waving a Starbucks gift card in front of my face.

"I don't know why, but I felt like I should give you this. Enjoy Starbucks on us today," he said.

It's little moments like this when I know that God uses the church to lift the heavy-hearted. Even if it's through a Starbucks gift card. And it shows me that God totally saw me and probably felt badly for me as I walked my freshman-butt back to my dorm. That was such a freshman thing for me to do, looking back on it, but I don't mean to make humor diminish this. If anyone can make fun of myself, it's me.

God saw how desperate I was for a church community, he saw my effort, and he rewarded it. After the gift card day, I started getting more involved in Crossroads, and meeting more and more people. He put me exactly where I was supposed to be, and he will do the very same for you.

My Church

I see my church as a straight up gift, and a great depiction of what church can look like.

I go to Crossroads Church in Oxford, Ohio, which is right next to my college. Every week, I look forward to seeing these bright and shiny faces welcome me. People actually know my name, not because of the reputation I built for myself, but rather because they care about me. It's nice to feel known and loved, right where you're at.

I could sit in any seat in that place, and I'd still feel welcome.

My church has come together to show others love. To be there for one another. And most importantly, to be there no matter how great my life is going, or how low I feel. My church is a constant, a lot like how Jesus is.

Some people may look at church as a weekly box to check off on the "good things I did this week" list. Maybe you're like me where you felt you were fulfilling a weekly obligation, even if you didn't pay attention to what the pastor said.

But going to church is so much more than fulfilling an obligation or enjoying free donuts after service. Church is a place to call home.

How to find your church

You might be like me and want to find a church to call home, but don't know where to begin. There really are a ton of churches to choose from. So if you are struggling to decide, follow the steps below.

1. Look around you

The best way to find a church is to look around you. Consider what is next to you geographically, something in your city. Maybe even if you've seen a church on social media, that could be an option for you as well. Maybe, if you're like me, you have friends around you who have found home in a specific church and you want to tag along and see what it's like. There are no rules about where to go, especially in this beginning stage where you are just beginning to dip your toes in the water of church - some people call this "church shopping", which while it is a funny thing to say, it is completely normal and healthy in finding your home. If you keep your ears and eyes open and are ready to receive an invitation to a church, you'll certainly find one.

2. Ask God to reveal where he wants you to be.

Whenever I don't know what to do, or I'm making a tough decision, I always look for answers from God. He is the ultimate question-answerer, the most prominent source of wisdom we have. He knows you better than you know yourself, and certainly wants to bless you with a community of people that you can call home and foster relationships with on Earth. He hears us and wants to answer any questions we have, and give us the direction we need, even if it's for what church to go to. We see this in the Bible as well: "Ask and it will be given to you; seek and you will find; knock and the door will be opened to you" (Matthew 7:7 NIV).

3. Where do you feel loved?

"You're already home where you feel loved," is a favorite lyric of mine ("Lost In My Mind" by the Head and The Heart) And this so darn true, especially when it comes to church. You're not going to want to join a church where you feel invisible or like no one cares about you.

There's nothing more beautiful than a group of people looking at you, knowing your name, and asking how you're doing, and actually caring about your response. It's special to have people who encourage you throughout your week and regularly pray for you- that is what the church is. Consider where you feel embraced, loved, and cared for, and go to this place. As one of my best friends would say, "Go where you are celebrated."

4. Where do you feel challenged?

A great church home is not only very welcoming, but also will provide a challenge. If you feel loved all the time but aren't really being challenged in anything, this isn't the best place to be. Although it is comfortable to be welcomed somewhere, God also designed us for growth. The goal is to go to a place where they are encouraging you and building you up, while also pointing you to be the person you can be. I love to learn, so I am always drawn to churches who give real-life insight to the Bible and deep viewpoints on life. Find a place where you feel challenged and encouraged.

Going To Church Alone

Alright, so at this point, you probably have a little bit of an idea of what church you want to go to. But you may run into a problem that I ran into, which is whom to go with. Some of my only Christian friends went with their families to church, and mine at the time wasn't exactly interested. I would have asked my current friends, but the thought of church did not sound too appealing to them. I didn't have a ton of Christian friends, so I was riding solo. Meaning, I had to go alone.

And I'll be honest, going to church alone is not the most comfortable thing. And by that I mean it sucked. I remember feeling like everyone was staring at me, thinking I was this weird loner. It sometimes felt like I was sitting alone at a lunch table in the middle of a room where everyone already had their friends. I was a table of one, a-one-man-team.

I, of course, always thought it was going to be this way.

But God knew otherwise. The other day at church, just four years after this lonely time, I found myself surrounded by all my best friends, brother, and mom at church. I was overwhelmed with how

God has given me people to live this faith journey with. He saw me four years ago when I felt alone, and he provided. He yearns to provide for you too.

You might feel weird right now going alone, but God is too good to have it stay that way. He designed us to not only be in relationship with Him, but to be in relationship with other people, and He delights in blessing you with that. He will give you friends to go to church with, people to share your faith with. But good things take time.

I promise you no one will stop talking or will stare at you as you open the doors and walk up the aisle, even though your imagination might think otherwise. People are much more focused on themselves to judge you for walking through the doors alone. Harsh, but true.

And when you go alone to church, God sees your faithfulness. And he loves to bless faithfulness. Keep going, and keep being brave. He will provide for you. But until then, walk with your head held high and your eyes open to a new community.

Serving In Church

If you're wanting to meet more people in your church, a great way to do so is by getting involved. This is a wonderful way to meet new people every week, and to be a part of a bigger mission.

At my church, there are so many different ways for people to get plugged into making service happen every week.

There's the first impressions team, where you welcome people and open doors. This one is my favorite because I love to smile and talk to people- classic, social-butterfly Ashley. If your church has an option for holding doors and greeting newcomers, and if you love people, I would highly recommend jumping into this role.

You can also serve on the music team. The first time I went to church, I felt this large push to join the worship band. Of course, this desire only lasted the duration of that morning and quickly faded with my after-church Tim Hortons iced capp, when I realized I was no Adele. It's funny when you think you're a good singer, and then you actually have to sing to real musical notes, and you soon see your singing career fly out the window. But if you have serious vocals or you love to play an instrument, I would really recommend looking into your church's worship team.

Not musically inclined and prefer not to socialize at the crack of dawn on a Sunday morning? Makes sense. There are tons of behind-the-scenes volunteer roles that could fit what you are looking for. Don't feel the need to be someone you are not - there is a place for you on the team whether you love talking to people, singing songs or not.

Among these options, there are a ton more ways to get involved in serving at your church. I recommend going to a couple of services and asking volunteers to direct you to different ways you can get involved and see what could be the right fit.

Online Sermons

Another great way to get involved in church is to watch and listen to sermons online. While I believe we should all have a physical church that we belong to, one we can go to with actual humans, there's something beautiful about being able to hear a powerful service that we can't see in person. Believe it or not, the online world has incredible resources to learn from and grow in your faith It is definitely a gift from God that we have that opportunity these days - so if that sounds interesting to you, look into it.

Now, with the help of the Internet, you can go to church any day of the week. Podcasts and YouTube have made it possible for incredible messages to be heard by more than the people sitting in the room listening to it live on a Sunday morning. We can stream these wonderful sermons to our phones or laptops - in the gym, while we get ready in the morning, or even in line at Starbucks. We can be reached by the Divine, even if it's through a screen.

Typically, I listen to sermons while I am working out. A sermon runs around one hour, so I am able to focus on the message instead of how much my legs hurt from Kayla Itsines BBG workout. There are so many sermons I have listened to, but there are a few that I would really recommend if you're just getting started with the online world of church.

Online sermons I love:

1. **Elevation Church with Steven Furtick:** This North Carolina church has a weekly podcast in which they stream the sermons, and I typically listen to the podcast on iTunes. Their online viewership is so large that they've actually named it their "e-fam". When I am not working out, I will look these up on their YouTube channel. I am telling you, these sermons are up in the millions of views for a reason. I have learned so much about the character of God through this church and the Lord has moved through these messages to reach me. Also, Steven Furtick is just awesome, so there's that.

2. **Transformation Church:** This church is led by an incredible pastor named Michael Todd. I found this church on YouTube through their sermons about living the single life. I would really recommend this church for spiritual growth. You can find their sermons on their YouTube channel.

3. **Crossroads Church -** I may be a little biased because this is the church I go to, but I can't lie that their sermons are flat-out amazing. This Midwest church focuses on those that have maybe given up on church, but not on God. They have their entire series on their website.

Application

Today, answer the questions above and pray about where you should go. Make a promise to yourself that whether you're going alone or not, walk through the doors of a church this week. Though it might be scary at first, God sees this act of faith, and he will not let that go overlooked. Your church home is out there - and it's just waiting for you to walk through its doors, take a seat, and enjoy the ride.

HOW TO SPEND YOUR MORNINGS

Mornings are hard for me. I, unfortunately, did not get the gene where you wake up on the first alarm and rise with a smile on your face, ready to take on your day. Instead, my mornings look more like letting my alarm go off five times and most likely sleeping through my first class.

Growing up, my mom tried several different tactics to get me out of bed. One of them involved opening up my blinds, and another involved her physically taking the covers off of me, like in the scene with Lindsay Lohan in *Freaky Friday*.

And if that didn't work, my dad would call up to my room and say, "Let me hear your feet on the floor." I kid you not, I would stomp ferociously for a couple of seconds, and then just like an undercover spy, I would hop back into bed.

One time after freshman year prom, I slept in my friend's bed until 3 o'clock. You read that right. And her grandpa had stopped by for most of the duration of that afternoon, and here's some girl named Ashley, completely dozed off in his granddaughter's room into the wee hours of the day.

So if you hate mornings, I want to tell you I am on your side. I feel your pain. No way am I going to step in here and tell you that I regularly wake up at 6am on the first alarm ring, birds chirping and sun shining like a Disney princess movie.

How "Quiet Time" Changed My Mornings

When I first got into my faith, I heard many Christians refer to their mornings as an opportunity for "quiet time". They would talk about spending the first 30 minutes of their morning in prayer, reading their Bible, or considering things they were grateful for. I was told that by spending the first minutes of my day with Jesus, I was able to have a much better outlook on the day and walk into any situation with purpose.

Of course, I didn't want to hate mornings forever, and this kind of morning sounded much more lovely than the chaotic, parents-yelling-at-me-to-get-up mornings that mine resembled. Rolling out of bed in the morning was not working too well for me, so I decided to try out this whole "quiet time" thing.

And let me tell you - my mornings were completely different. I actually was excited to wake up a bit earlier because I saw how much of a positive impact this had on my day.

I spent the first part of my morning diving through a devotional, which walked me through a message a day and would end with journaling and prayer. See the end of the chapter for some of my favorite devotionals that you could try.

Every day I did the devotional, I would look at my day with intentionality. I considered the people I wanted to love, the situations I wanted to work hard in, and what I was struggling with that I wanted to let God into that day. Through this time, God was able to equip me for all of these different aspects of my day and give me strength to face anything that came my way.

The more I made quiet time a priority in my morning, the more affected I was when I would skip a morning. I found myself feeling anxious, distracted, and less motivated. And even more prominent was my impatience with annoying people. Because I could notice the difference of a day with Jesus in the morning versus a day without him, I started to make this time a regular part of my day-to-day life. It was food for my spirit.

I have found that spending time with Jesus in the morning is the perfect way for me to go into the day with confidence. It's a way for me to re-center and create a focus for the day. Instead of rolling out of bed and into my day without purpose, I can be intentional about what I am pursuing that day and am reminded of what's really important in life.

What Is Quiet Time?

"Quiet time" is another way to describe spending time with God. It can also be described as a time when you "quiet" your mind to his words and presence.

As for where you should go for this time, it might be distracting doing your quiet time where others can see you. I know when I find myself doing this in front of others, I always feel self-conscious.

So for starters, I would practice this in the quiet of your room. Spending time with Jesus in your room is a private experience and allows you to focus directly on your time with Him without any interruptions.

I usually stay in my room and sit on my bed while I do this. I typically try to make my bed before I do my quiet time, that way I don't fall asleep in the midst of talking to Jesus and sleep through my classes, which is much more possible for me than you would think.

And as for when you should start your quiet time, I find it's best done before any other distractions. I'm talking about before checking Instagram, before responding to group messages, before reading emails. The best way to start your morning is in the presence of Jesus, your biggest advocate and cheerleader. He provides much more peace than any kind of social media can.

There is no distinct amount of time you should spend in a quiet time - you can take as long as you want. While you are getting the hang of this, I would try to wake up 20 to 30 minutes earlier in the morning to give yourself time. I can feel you rolling your eyes when I say that, and I almost did too. But if you make yourself a cup of coffee, it will be a lot more bearable, and maybe even peaceful.

My routine goes a little like this: I wake up, shower, throw on makeup and a cute outfit, and eat breakfast. I am basically ready for my day, and my last step is my quiet time, which I give myself around 10-20 minutes for. I try my very hardest to not get on my phone before I am done with quiet time. If I do anything on my phone, it's to listen to some good music to wake me up.

Now that I'm 5 years into regular quiet times, I've figured out a morning routine that works wonders for me, and it could for you too. Check out the three steps I take every morning in my quiet time.

Step 1: Gratitude

To start my quiet time, I begin by thanking God for what He's given me. I thank God for things he's given me currently, and what he's provided for in the past. So for example, I thank God for the positive mindset he's given me through this tough season of my life. I thank God for my new counselor, my parents, a good night of sleep, even my health. Sometimes I thank him for how cozy my room is, or how yummy my coffee is. There are no limits to gratitude.

A challenge I have for you is to say three different things you are thankful for each day. And you can't repeat any item, so eventually, you have to get creative about it.

Gratitude is a great way to start your day because you are beginning with a posture of appreciation. Instead of immediately thinking about what you need from God, you start out reflecting on what He has already given you.

Step 2: Prayer

Prayer is a time to talk to God about the day ahead and ask for any help needed. In my quiet time, I usually tell him what's on my mind for that day, whether it's about a person, struggle or situation. I will talk to him like he's a friend about whatever is on my mind, and I will ask him for help with each situation.

I then will pray for other people in my life. I'll ask God to bless my family and I'll ask God to intervene in ways for other people.

I'll then ask him to give me strength for the day. If I need patience, strength, peace, a stronger belief in Him - I will ask him to provide what I need.

Prayer is simple. You can just talk to God, about your day and your worries, and ask him for specific help in these situations. You can also ask him to help other people in your life.

If you want to take your prayer to the next level, you can pray for our country, for an end to racism, for our government, the homeless man you saw on the street, the stock market - you name it. Just like there are no limits to gratitude, there are also no limits to prayer.

Step 3: Reading and Writing

This is the last and final step of your quiet time. In this time, you can read books of scripture as we talked about in the chapter before, or you can read a devotional.

In the first year of my faith, devotionals had an incredible impact on my life. A devotional is a book that splits different biblical concepts into chapters, and you will typically read one chapter a day. Each chapter contains a bible verse to read, and then an explanation from the author about the verse. It then closes with a prayer. It can take 5 to 10 minutes to read a chapter, depending on the book.

There are many amazing devotionals to choose from. Below is a list of devotionals that I would suggest for the beginning of your faith journey:

- The Blue Book- This was my first devotional, and I couldn't recommend it enough. This book provides an in-depth look at different topics addressed in the Bible, like finding direction, trusting God with your future, or coping with anxiety. Each chapter walks you through a different concept in the Bible and how it relates to life, with excerpts and anecdotes from deep, thought-provoking stories. If you love to learn and are yearning to dig into God's truth, I would recommend this resource as a great start.

- First 5 app - This app has several Bible studies to choose from and takes you day by day through a biblical story, and the message behind it. This is an app from an incredible women's ministry called Proverbs 31, and it's *free*, so what's not to love about that? This one takes no more than 5 minutes a day and can be the "first 5" minutes of your day. It also provides several different reading plans on several books of the Bible. It also has a comments section for each devotional, where you can then see how other users were affected by the reading. I've been walking through this for the last couple months and love it.

- Jesus Calling - This is a very popular devotional that is less than $10. This is written specifically for women, so there are a lot of topics that are very relatable. This devotional contains one page a day, with a Bible verse, an encouraging message, and a closing prayer. Though this book is very simple, it can have a huge impact. I have met so many people who have been going through something and flipped to a page of this devotional which spoke directly to that struggle. This book has touched many hearts, and the author has such a good understanding of how the Gospel can impact our daily lives.

- Love God Greatly - I just discovered this app and it has made a huge impact on my life. This is a free resource that has several different plans to walk you through, from the "Promises of God" to dealing with fear. I love this resource because there is always a relatable story paired with scripture, and the words always fuel me with encouragement for the day.

I hope with the addition of quiet time, you can enjoy your mornings a little bit more than you did before. I know now I am less inclined to snooze, and more inclined to get out of bed and start my day. Of course, I still have my days when the snooze button is tempting - but I've learned that starting my day in God's presence is a whole lot more enjoyable than a few extra minutes of shuteye.

Quiet time has just about changed the way I start my day, and given me a whole different sense of meaning for even the smallest tasks. Starting our days with Jesus can help us feel like we are walking into our lives with purpose, no matter how ordinary life may feel.

Application

This week, I encourage you to start doing a regular quiet time. Pick a devotional you'd want to read from, maybe even choose one of the guides mentioned above. Try to wake up just 20 minutes earlier than normal, grab yourself a yummy cup of coffee, and sit in the quiet of your room. Practice the three steps we went over above, and see how God moves in your day to day life. Your mornings are about to get a whole lot sweeter.

ALL ABOUT SMALL GROUP

If you told me six years ago to go to a bible study, I would've shut you down. This kind of thing seemed terrifying to me, because I didn't know anything about the Bible, nor did I want to be in a room with people that made me feel stupid. I also conjured up an idea that the girls who go to Bible study are perfect and never make any mistakes and never say any cuss words, and I did not belong in such an atmosphere.

Looking back on this thought process, I certainly had a pretty distorted view of what a Bible study is really like.

For a while, I was only comfortable talking about Jesus and reading the Bible with only my mentor. She was kind, inviting, and funny, and that was all I needed in a Christian friend. As a matter of fact, I figured I could do well with only one friend to share my faith with.

But this friendship didn't change the fact that I was pretty lonely at the beginning of my faith. I didn't have many friends to confide in, and I'm sure a bible study could've been a place where I would meet some good friends who could encourage me in my faith journey.

Once I got to college, I was more open to the idea of joining a bible study. I also heard people calling this a "small group", which seemed much less scary. I didn't know if I could study the Bible, but I certainly could go to a group that is on the smaller side.

Since high school wasn't too great for me in the friend category, I knew I wanted things to be different in college. But I also knew that to actually make this happen, I needed to get out of my comfort zone and get my booty to a place with people trying to grow in their faith as well. Even if that meant I didn't know anyone, or if I needed to join eight different groups, I would go until I found one that worked. This is how desperate I was for a community.

Thankfully, a friend told me about a small group in the first week of college. The group was hosted at a house and led by older, wiser seniors at my school. I was nervous on the car ride there, but once I walked through the door and felt the welcoming warmth of that living room, my fear washed away.

With each week, I felt more and more comfortable to ask questions and talk about different topics. These nights were spent opening up about life and hearing about the different predicaments we were all facing. I learned the power of women supporting other women in that room.

Not only that, but I met one of my best friends through this group. God used one bold step of faith to provide for me. If I had stayed comfortable and played it safe, I would not have the best friends that I do today.

After freshman year, I joined a sorority and started a small group with my chapter. But to be honest, barely anyone ever came, and it wasn't very well-structured. Since we wanted it to keep going, we let anyone come who wanted to, and many girls from other chapters made it part of their weekly routine.

The group that was meant for only my sorority then expanded to other sororities. With each week, the group got bigger and bigger, and more girls from different chapters were walking through our doors. Soon enough, we got to the point where almost 30 girls from Greek life were piling into a room and talking about Jesus and their lives. We certainly didn't plan for this to happen, but it has become such an incredible place for people to have community and to feel like they belong.

Why join a small group?

The purpose of a small group is to build community and to provide a space for encouraging each other and pointing each other to Jesus. I see small group as one, big therapy session - but with Jesus and laughter at the core.

These people will eventually be your people. The girls that actually know what's going on in your life, instead of staying at a superficial level. They will pray for you when you're in tears, and they will help you get back on your own two feet when life has knocked you down. And you're able to do the same for them.

They can also help you with serious decisions, or wisdom on a subject. I'll be honest, half my problems wouldn't be solved if it weren't for the lovely input of my small group.

Bible study is a place to find friends, to find purpose, and to find more of Jesus. And what's not to love about that?

As much as we are studying the Bible, the friendships made through this time together is the best perk to these groups. You get to have a place where people actually support you, know what's going on in your life, and will laugh and cry with you (maybe even at the same time, as this can happen).

How do I find one to join?

There are many different ways to find a small group. You might know someone who knows someone who is leading a small group, and this is something to consider attending.

And chances are, your church will present an opportunity to join a group. At my church, they have a whole hub where you can search for a Bible study that works for you and fits with your stage of life.

It's kind of like online dating, but Bible study dating. Brilliant concept.

Put the word out to your church community or any Christian friends that you want to join a small group, and this will better your chances of getting involved.

I recommend joining a small group of likeminded gals, so if you are in high school, it's best to join one with other high schoolers. If you're in college, it's best to join one with other college women. This way you are able to walk through the same season of life together and support each other while experiencing it.

I'm terrified to go. What if I don't know anything?

I can absolutely promise you that no one is going to call on you, make you stand up and recite the 10 commandments. Of course, this was one of my irrational thoughts, but sometimes our perception of how things are going to go can be influenced by fear.

I didn't think I was good enough or smart enough to walk into one of these groups. But truth is, these groups are not meant to embarrass you or quiz you on the Bible. There will be no tests. Instead, there will be open arms, inviting faces, and loud laughter.

This is a place for you to learn at your own pace about who Jesus is and open up about your life. It's a place to feel loved and to seek guidance. It's a place to be supported and challenged, and to do the same for others. By stepping into this space, you're able to see God move and work in your life and the lives of others, and you'll see how scripture can transform lives.

I will tell you that even if you are shy, there is something beautiful about stepping out of your comfort zone and going to one of these groups. And if courage seems lacking, try to ask someone to go with you. When we have someone go with us to one of these things, we feel so much more prepared to tackle it.

If you're wondering how much you should talk, you can talk as much as you like. And on the contrary, you can listen as much as you want. I've noticed that in bible study, you're either more of a listener or more of a talker. And the group needs both. Do not feel any pressure to talk during the group, you can feel comfortable to just sit and be. But if you feel an urge to say something, go for it.

What should I expect?

Usually, small groups happen weekly on the same night and will be hosted at the same place. This can either be a living room of a house or in a church setting. The ones I've gone to have been in really comfortable settings, with couches and pillows and blankets, which makes the experience much more worthwhile.

With the small groups I've gone to, you all pile into one room and the first couple of minutes is just about getting comfortable. Then after some chit chat, the leader will take it from there and probably ask some general questions about everyone's weeks. With my groups, we've usually all gone around the room and said a "peach and a pit". The peach is a good part of the week, and the pit is the bad part. It's a great way to get to know people and what they deal with on a day-to-day basis. You can go as deep as you want with this, and since it's your first time, it's okay if you don't reveal your whole life story to these people. Trust can take time.

After peaches and pits, we usually start off with a passage in the Bible. If you don't have a Bible, you can just share with someone there, or just use an app on your phone (The Bible app is a great resource for this). The group will usually "popcorn" read the passage, when one person will read a couple of verses, then another will read the next verses.

After the reading is done, usually the group has a big conversation about the passage. You can talk about what stood out to you, any questions you have, and what was confusing. Usually, someone will mention how this scripture applies to their life, and that can be a great way to spur a conversation.

After chatting for a while, the leader will close in prayer. This is a great time to get out any prayer requests. I'd encourage you to go deep with this, because the more vulnerable you are with the group, the closer the group will get to you. I know it's scary to be honest about what you need prayer for, but it's beautiful when people start to encourage you in that space and actually know what's going on in your life. And you can do the same for them.

And then if there are cookies there, go grab yourself a cookie. And voila! You are done with your first small group.

Application

If you know about a group that is meeting this next week, I encourage you to get yourself there. I know, Netflix sounds a lot better than going to a place where you may not know anyone. But if you go and you hate it, you've lost absolutely nothing. But if you go and you love it, well, you've certainly gained more than watching an extra hour of TV.

If you can get through middle school, you can certainly make it through your first day at small group (middle school was the worst thing I could think of at the moment, so bear with me.) When we step out in faith, even if it's through the doors of a small group leader's home, we will certainly be rewarded. And who knows? Your new best friend could be right around the corner, with one tiny ounce of courage.

I HAVE A BIBLE - BUT WHAT DO I DO WITH IT?

If you've never opened one, the Bible can seem like a mystery. To be honest, I didn't start reading the Bible until a year into my faith journey, because I was scared of it. And I want for you to dig into this gem a lot sooner than I did, because it's really not as scary as it may seem.

I bought my Bible with the friend that introduced me to Jesus. We took a good ole trip to Barnes and Noble and went right to the Bible section, and I got a cute green one with a yellow flower on it. This is something most Christians don't tell you, but the cuter it is, the more you'll read it.

Even though mine was as adorable as can be, it still rested snug on my shelf. I didn't open it at all.

I remember to this day staring at it on my shelf in my childhood bedroom and being so intimidated. I thought that if I opened it, I would be directed to another language, like Latin, or maybe a light beam would shoot out of it. Or maybe I was afraid it would be boring and I wouldn't understand a word.

I didn't know the power of this book, and I was scared that I wasn't smart enough or "spiritual" enough to unleash it.

Thankfully, God knew I was intimidated, so he sent some help. This came in the form of my friend Layne, who became a mentor in my life. I met her through a Young Life meeting and immediately felt like we would be best friends, despite her being four years older than me. We connected on so many levels, and I looked up to her. (My hope is that each of you can find your Layne, someone who is just a few steps ahead of you in your faith to help you in your journey, and to cry with you through life's storms. In fact, when my life hits the fan, I still go to her, and she welcomes me into her home with opened arms and a box of tissues.)

Layne and I would grab coffee together, and this is where she would help me read the Bible. Oddly enough, we had the same Bible, with the same yellow flower on it, and we didn't even know it. God has quite a sense of humor.

Layne showed me the roadmap to reading the Bible, which I am about to show you below.

But first - let's get down to the essentials.

Why should I read the Bible?

Maybe you don't think the Bible is that important, and I was in your shoes, so I don't blame you. I wanted to just talk to Jesus all day, and feel the Holy Spirit in my life, but I didn't want to read a boring book about weird stories that happened thousands of years ago. That idea just didn't seem appealing to me.

But I realized that without the Bible, our relationship with Jesus can only go so far. I heard that the Bible is like a love letter from God to us. We see more of his character, his grace, and his love for us weird humans in the many pages of this book.

Two years after I thought the Bible was a boring old book, I can confidently tell you these pages have changed my life. I have learned more about who I am when I was feeling worthless. I have learned about God's security when my life was falling apart. I have overcome by his peace when he's led me to words that I needed to hear, to let me know I was going to be okay. His Word has transformed me, and I want that for you too.

What is the Bible?

The Bible is a collection of books written over thousands of years all telling God's story from one family tree, with many different authors.

The first book is Genesis, the last book is Revelation. Each book is a story about God. Some books are more read than others - for example, many people read the book of Philippians before they read the book of Zephaniah. Do I know what the book of Zephaniah is about? Nope, I certainly do not, but I hope one day I will.

The Bible is composed of two different sections - the Old Testament (before the birth of Jesus) and the New Testament (after Jesus' birth).

The Old Testament of the Bible begins with the book of Genesis - which tells the story of Adam and Eve. These were the first male and female, who were made in God's image to rule over the world and to experience a perfect relationship with God. After sin enters the world, the rest of the Old Testament contains stories about the imperfection of humans and their struggle with good and evil. Meanwhile, we see God in the work of delivering them from this bondage, and to rebuild his connection with his people.

The rest of the Old Testament follows people who were all in one genealogy, so one "family tree", which all led to Jesus Christ, the ultimate deliverer of humans. In the Old Testament, we see stories about Moses, David, Abraham, and other biblical heroes in Jesus's genealogy.

After the Old Testament ends, the New Testament begins. The New Testament is towards the end of the Bible - and these books are all about Jesus.

The first four books are the "Gospels" which tell Jesus's story on earth through four different perspectives: Matthew, Mark, Luke, and John. The rest of the New Testament is mostly written by the Apostle Paul, who was a follower of Jesus after he died, and other authors. There is an author behind every book of the Bible.

Okay, so I totally want a Bible - where do I get one?

There are so many places to get a good-ole Bible. I got mine at Barnes and Noble, and they have plenty of ones to choose from. Wherever you go, I recommend getting a newer translation. Some great translations are the New International Version (NIV) or the New Living Translation (NLT) because these are the most modern and popular translations. AKA: You can actually understand what the heck is going on.

If you've noticed, I've added some verses in here that are cited as MSG version. This version is basically a modern-day translation of the Bible. I don't know many Bibles transcribed in this, but you can find this version on some of the iPhone apps listed below.

Here's an example of the difference between an old translation and a new translation. I'll show you one of my favorite verses in an older translation - one you would see in traditional mass (King James Version (KJV)) and newer translation (New International Version (NIV) - one you would see on Pinterest).

New International Version (NIV)

"Do not be anxious about anything, but in every situation, by prayer and petition, with thanksgiving, present your requests to God." (Philippians 4:6 NIV)

King James Version (KJV)

Be careful for nothing; but in every thing by prayer and supplication with thanksgiving let your requests be made known unto God. (Philippians 4:6 KJV)

Hold up - I don't even know what supplication means. See what I'm saying? If you are a King James advocate - I do not want you to stop loving what you love. But for those of you starting out in your faith journey, I recommend getting this translation, NIV. If you want two other good options, NLT or ESV are also great. I've used the NIV version for years and loved it.

Links to some of my favorite Bibles:

- She Reads Truth Bible - A cute Bible that is less than $30, with adorable verses and art, and custom Bible studies to different books.
- Hosanna Revival Bible - These Bibles are painted and so adorable. It's also a local business in Cincinnati - and I think we should all #supportlocal.
- Journal the Word Bible - Love note-taking? This Bible leaves all the room for your heart's content to do some good ole' journaling.

And about spending money on these Bibles - I know they are not cheap. But this is a very, very important book in your life - if not, the most important. So skip the pair of shoes in your Nordstrom's cart and instead put that money toward a Bible you love.

I don't understand why people call them verses. Are verses quotes? What the heck.

I get this struggle. Verses and quotes are not the same things, even though for a whole year I called a verse "my favorite quote". I want to free you from any Christian humiliation.

Bible verses are called "scripture", and people refer to a line from the bible as a "verse". When you are reading the Bible, there will be numbers next to the verses so you can better track them, and find these verses whenever. Though this may sound confusing now, this will all make sense in the next couple of pages.

Let's take a Bible verse and pick it apart together.

How to read a Bible verse

Let's start with Philippians 4:6, a very popular Bible verse about anxiety that was mentioned above.

1. Find the book: In this case, Philippians is the book in which the verse is located. If you want to find any book, look in the table of contents of your bible, which will save you a whole lot of page flipping.
2. Find the chapter: So what is 4:6? These numbers may look intimidating, but they are there to direct you to the specific chapter and place where the verse is located. Since the next step is to find the chapter - the chapter is always the first number you see. In this case, we are in Philippians chapter 4.
3. Finding the verse: The second number, 6, is where the verse is in that chapter. So after you have gone to the 4th chapter, you can then go to the 6th verse, which you can find by looking at the numbers. The numbers are always in chronological order.

Again:
Philippians 4:6
Philippians   4:   6
^ book   ^ chapter #   ^ verse number in chapter

Now, let's put this to practice. Here's an excerpt of the first part of Philippians 4. The numbers you see next to the sentences are the verse numbers (where the second number of your verse is put to use)

Philippians 4: New International Version (NIV)

1 Therefore, my brothers and sisters, you whom I love and long for, my joy and crown, stand firm in the Lord in this way, dear friends! 2 I plead with Euodia and I plead with Syntyche to be of the same mind in the Lord. 3 Yes, and I ask you, my true companion, help these women since they have contended at my side in the cause of the gospel, along with Clement and the rest of my co-workers, whose names are in the book of life.

4 Rejoice in the Lord always. I will say it again: Rejoice! 5 Let your gentleness be evident to all. The Lord is near. 6 **Do not be anxious about anything, but in every situation, by prayer and petition, with thanksgiving, present your requests to God.** 7 And the peace of God, which transcends all understanding, will guard your hearts and your minds in Christ Jesus.

See where the verse is we pointed to at the beginning of the chapter? We found the chapter, then the verse. Good job! When we want to find a verse, we go through these three steps:

1. Find the book in the table of contents. In this case, find Philippians.
2. Flip to the chapter of the book, which in this case, is chapter 4.
3. In chapter 4, look for the verse number - which is the 6th verse.

So now you know how to pick apart a Bible verse - let's dig into how do you actually start reading the Bible.

The best books to start reading today

(If you want to know where these books are, look to your Table of Contents. It will save you a lot of page flipping.)

1. The Gospel of John: If you're a new believer, the best place to start is the book of John. This is the story of Jesus's life written by one of his disciples, or shall I say "besties", John. John saw all the miracles Jesus did and got to know him on a personal level. He describes what Jesus was all about, and what he wants for our own lives.
2. Romans: This is my favorite book of the Bible. It is full of so much hope. This book is a great place to start to get full of knowledge about what God wants for his people, and what the life of Jesus means for us.
3. James: This is a book of only four chapters written by Jesus's brother, James. This book is full of wisdom and perseverance, and a great place to start.

How on earth do I read these books?

When I started reading the Bible, I started at the beginning with Genesis, and I tried to read it all in one sitting. This I would not recommend. I was quickly bored, confused and scared. Probably because after Adam and Eve screw up and eat the apple, it all pretty much goes downhill, with wars and battles and death. Lots of death.

Thank God for Layne, who redirected my attention. Not to say that Genesis isn't full of great stuff, it's just not what you might want to read at the beginning of your journey, because it's on the weirder, harder-to-follow side.

If you want to learn more about Jesus and his love for you, I'd start out in a book that tells his story, which would be any of the four Gospels (Matthew, Mark, Luke or John). A "Gospel" tells the story of Christ.

And as for how much to read, I'd recommend reading a couple of nuggets a day. It's best to take the reading in doses. For example, maybe read a chapter a day of a book. If that is too long, because some chapters can be longer than others (take Romans for example), you can just read a chunk of verses at a time, until you feel satisfied. Maybe that's six verses a day.

Whatever it is, don't feel bad that you are not reading more, because I have found the less scripture I read, the more I get out of it. There is no rush here - you have the rest of your life to read God's word, and you'll be surprised how much you can take away from just a couple of verses.

You can read the Bible in the morning before you start your day, or you can read it before bed. If you want some help understanding the Bible, devotionals are a great place to start. There are several devotionals out there that will take you through a book of the Bible and dissect what the verses are saying, and how it applies to your day to day life.

Memorizing scripture

I urge you to memorize scripture. It's crazy that when I take the time to memorize scripture, I feel so much peace move through me. I think it's because I am spending the time to meditate on words of truth, which is like water for a parched spirit, encouragement for a downcast soul.

Memorizing scripture can come in handy in your day to day life. For example, if you feel insecure, the Holy Spirit might throw the verse in your head "You are fearfully and wonderfully made" (Psalm 139:14).

You had to memorize it first, but now God can use that to remind you of what is true when you can't immediately believe it yourself.

By memorizing verses, you give yourself more access to truth during the day. And that is friggin awesome. It is one of the coolest things to be thinking about something, and then have a verse pop in your head that directly goes with your situation. That is by no accident, my friend.

And good news, there's an app for memorizing bible verses. If you download the "Verses" app, it helps you memorize pieces of scripture through games, sort of like Quizlet. But so much better than Quizlet.

If you don't want to use the app, you can just write the verses out again and again on a notecard, until you know it by heart.

To start, here are some verses I would recommend memorizing:

- Jeremiah 29:11 - "'For I know the plans I have for you,' declares the Lord, "plans to prosper you and not to harm you, plans to give you hope and a future."
- Romans 8:28 - "And we know that in all things God works for the good of those who love him, who have been called according to his purpose."

- Psalms 139:14 - "I praise you because I am fearfully and wonderfully made; your works are wonderful, I know that full well."
- James 1: 2-4 - "Consider it pure joy, my brothers and sisters, whenever you face trials of many kinds, because you know that the testing of your faith produces perseverance. Let perseverance finish its work so that you may be mature and complete, not lacking anything."
- Philippians 4:6 - "Do not be anxious about anything, but in everything, by prayer and petition, submit your requests to God. And the peace of God, which transcends all understanding, will guard your hearts and your minds in Christ Jesus."
- Philippians 4:13 - "I can do all things through Christ who strengthens me."

Some Bible reading resources I can't live without:

As well as the Verses app, I also find these tools very helpful in reading the Bible:
- The Bible Project YouTube Channel: I cannot tell you how many times these videos have helped me understand the stories of the Bible. This popular YouTube channel (with over a million subscribers) gives you access to different videos that explain stories of the Bible in an illustrative, engaging way. Go give the Proverbs one a try, and you'll see what I'm talking about.
- SheReadsTruth app: This app gives you full on access to the Bible in several different translations. They have the Message (MSG) translation here, which contains wording that emulates the way we talk in the 21st century.
- Thesaurus: I am kind of a word geek if you cannot already tell. But sometimes if I come across a word, I look it up on Thesaurus.com and I can get a better understanding of the word.
- Bible Dictionary: This is an excellent resource for getting down to the historical and cultural context of a book. I don't use this resource too often, but there are many times when it comes in handy.

- DesiringGod.com: This is a website created by John Piper, a successful pastor, and leader. In this website, you'll find several articles about different pieces of scripture, sometimes even paired with a related sermon. If you want to dig into a book, I recommend searching the book's name in the search bar and navigate the different resources available.
- The Bible app: This is another resource to dig more into the Bible, right from your phone screen, and with zero charge.
- A mentor: Okay, so this is not something you can instantly get by the touch of a download button. I wish that was the case because that would be awesome. But seriously, I don't know where I would be without Layne, my Young Life leader, in that first year of my faith journey. Whenever I had a question about what I was reading in the Bible, i.e. slavery which totally pissed me off, she was a quick call away. And sometimes, we would even read Scripture together and unpack it, which made me feel more comfortable and confident to read the Bible on my own.

All in all, I know God wants a mentor for you. I encourage you to pray for one, pray for a like-minded person who is just a couple steps ahead of you in their faith, who can help you in your faith journey. Pray for this, and then keep your eyes open for any potential suitors.

My hope is that through reading the Bible, you can learn more about God's love for you and his story of redemption. Though it's an act of courage to open one up, there is a whole world of wisdom in the pages of God's Word for us humans. Wisdom that will not only give you direction, but will change how you see yourself, life, and God. If you let it, this wisdom just might change your life.

Application

This week, I encourage you to go get yourself a Bible. Bring a friend for support, just so you don't end up picking an ugly one. After you pick one up, practice finding the verse Philippians 4:13, which says "I can do all things through Christ who strengthens me." You can follow the steps we went over in this chapter to find it. And then once you've found it, try to memorize this scripture. I know these are a bunch of big steps, but I totally believe in you, or else I wouldn't be asking these things of you. I think these steps will help you get over the hump of opening up the Bible and getting rid of any feelings of inadequacy, just like they did for me. I can't wait for you to dig into the most beautiful love letter you'll ever read.

GIVE ME A W FOR WORSHIP

Worship is a term that may be confusing for the beginner Christian, as it was kind of confusing for me. The google definition for Worship is:

"the feeling or expression of reverence and adoration for a deity."

So basically, worship can be anything that you are doing for God, or out of love for God.

How Do I Worship?

There is no perfect way to worship. But a tried and true way is to listen to worship music. There are classic Christian songs, and then there's more contemporary music. There are some absolutely wonderful songs to worship to, that have a wonderful melody and are really soulful. If you love music, you are in luck, because it is a beautiful way to feel the presence of God.

You can worship anywhere, and certainly not just in church. I jam out to worship music in the car, while doing homework, and even in the shower.

The car is my most frequent worship session, and I am positive I've received some concerning looks at the stoplight. I have raised my hands in the car and everything, people probably thought I was trying to signal something on the road. Oh, well.

I am a huge fan of music. It is a part of my daily medicine of life-with-Ashley, along with books and the love of Jesus. Music is a great way for me to adore God and be in awe of his work and presence in my life.

Worship Song Suggestions

I have a "Go Jesus" playlist, so I recommend making a playlist with your own flare.

If you're like me, you might want to have some song suggestions. Song suggestions might be one of my favorite things to hear. So here are some songs and worship bands I recommend listening to:

- Hillsong Worship
  - Favorite songs: "I Am Who You Say I Am", "Seasons", "The Passion", "New Wine", "So Will I"
- Elevation Worship
  - "Do It Again", "O Come To The Altar", "Here Again", "Won't Stop Now", "None"
- Bethel Music (This band does a ton of songs with other singers. I recommend downloading the entire "You Make Me Brave" album, it is a masterpiece)
  - "Shepherd", "Pieces", "You Make Me Brave", "Come To Me", "Wonder", "It Is Well"
- Lauren Daigle
  - "How Can It Be", "Still Rolling Stones", "Trust In You", "Look Up Child"
- Other individual songs I love:
  - "Out Of Hiding" by Stephanie Gretzinger
  - "Surrounded (Fight My Battles)" by Michael W. Smith
  - "Worthy of it all (All of the glory)" by UPPERROOM
  - "Beautiful Surrender" by Jonathan David and Melissa Helser
  - "Reckless Love" by Cory Asbury
  - "Come Thou Fount" by Kings (MHM)

Is music the only way to worship? Certainly not!

The Apostle Paul says this in Romans:

"Therefore, I urge you, brothers and sisters, in view of God's mercy, to offer your bodies as a living sacrifice, holy and pleasing to God-- this is your true and proper worship." (Romans 12:1, NIV)

The message version describes this verse like this:

"So here's what I want you to do, God helping you: Take your everyday, ordinary life—your sleeping, eating, going-to-work, and walking-around life—and place it before God as an offering. Embracing what God does for you is the best thing you can do for him. Don't become so well-adjusted to your culture that you fit into it without even thinking. Instead, fix your attention on God. You'll be changed from the inside out." (Romans 12:1-2, MSG)

What he is saying here is that anything you do for God can count as an act of worship. I find that doing things we love can be a way of worshipping God. For me, I love to read and write, so many times I find myself worshipping God when I am doing these things.

I know some people who love to run, and you might wonder how on earth could that be a thing, but running can be a form of worship they give to God.

Anything you do can be done for God. You can love someone for God, maybe it's someone who really rubs you the wrong way. You can thank God every time you order your favorite Starbucks, and you can love and encourage the barista for God. You can pet your dog for God. You can drive to work, or walk to class, for God. If you do it with the intention of looking to God and honoring him with your life, this is a "true and proper worship".

Using your gifts as an act of worship

Another way I've seen worship is when someone uses their gifts as a way to give back to God. For example, writing this book is an act of worship, because I am doing it out of God's love for me, and the gift he's given me to be able to put words together in nice, meaningful sentences.

It doesn't matter how small the job is, when it is done for God, it counts as an act of worship. Paul even directs us to do our work in God's name, no matter if you are at the top of the corporate ladder or just doing what you love as a hobby.

This reminds me of the story of the street sweeper from Martin Luther King Jr:

And when you discover what you will be in your life, set out to do it as if God Almighty called you at this particular moment in history to do it.

Don't just set out to do a good job. Set out to do such a good job that the living, the dead or the unborn couldn't do it any better.

If it falls your lot to be a street sweeper, sweep streets like Michelangelo painted pictures, sweep streets like Beethoven composed music, sweep streets like Leontyne Price sings before the Metropolitan Opera. Sweep streets like Shakespeare wrote poetry.

Sweep streets so well that all the hosts of heaven and earth will have to pause and say: Here lived a great street sweeper who swept his job well.

When we do things like God called us to do, we are able to give him all the glory and perform our best. Even if it as simple as sweeping the streets.

Gratitude as worship

I've found that another way to be in awe of God is to be grateful for what you have. They say that every good and perfect gift is from above, so anything you have in life that makes you smile is a gift from God. It is good for our hearts to thank God for providing for us.

We can be thankful for so many things. I find it's human nature to focus on what you need, instead of putting your attention on what you already have. But I will say that once we shift our attention to being grateful for what we have, this is the sweet spot.

Gratitude is the key to joy. It's a beautiful thing to take the time to thank God every day for what you have because he is responsible for the blessing. Maybe you're grateful for your family and friends, but you can also be grateful for the sun, you can be grateful for books. Worship can be in the confines of looking to God and saying, "Thank you. You're awesome." And what a beautiful posture to have.

Your worship doesn't have to look like everybody else's

Believe it or not, church is not the only place for worship. You can worship anywhere, through the beauty of music, ordering Starbucks, using your talents, or being grateful for what you have. It's as simple as that.

Application

This week, I'd encourage you to practice worship in one way. Whether that's jamming out to one of the songs listed above, or ordering your coffee as an act of worship, there is nothing you can't do out of honor for God.

HOW TO FIND COMMUNITY

I'll be honest - when I became a Christian, I only had one friend to confide in about my faith. That was it. Though I was excited about my new discovery, it wasn't enough to take away my loneliness.

My high school friend group never talked about Jesus, and they mainly thought people in Young Life were weirdos. Though I had a few good friends in high school, it was difficult not having a faith community.

It gave me hope when I met the friends my Young Life leader had in college. At Ohio State, she had an array of supportive, encouraging women around her who helped her grow in her faith. When I visited her, I saw the warmth of the friendships she had, the way they treated each other, the laughter they shared.

I saw the power of women building each other up, pointing each other to Jesus, and being honest with one another. I prayed that though I didn't have that at the time, that one day God would bless me with this kind of community in college.

No matter where you are at, you can have a clean slate.

It is never too late to look for a new community, to befriend someone new, to get yourself out there.

Maybe part of the reason you were attracted to this whole Jesus thing is the kindness you saw at how Christian friends treat each other, as opposed to your friends who gossip the entire time you are together. Maybe people don't even ask you how your day was, or you feel like you never quite say the right thing, walking on eggshells. Maybe you just feel completely out of place.

But good news, my friend. Jesus loves to redeem heartbreak, loneliness, and bad situations.

Four years after crying myself to sleep some nights because of my lack of a faith community, I now have countless besties who build me up and point me to Jesus. I have been provided with a sweeter community than I could have ever imagined. God has given me the kind of friends I saw Him give my mentor Layne, and what a gift they are. I hope my story can give you confidence that he will show up for you, and you will not be lonely forever.

In the meantime, there are things you can do to increase the likelihood at getting plugged into community.

Get Yourself Out There

To have a friend, you need to be a friend. If you find that you feel lonely, you can reach out to someone. Instead of waiting for friends to come knocking on your door, extend the invitation first.

Watching five episodes of *This Is Us* in your dorm is not going to get you any friends. Even though this is one heck of a show, and yes, I have totally done this once or twice. But unfortunately, being in a cocoon isn't the best magnet for new friendships.

Friendship requires effort. It takes getting out of your own comfort zone, and the best way to get out of your comfort zone is to get involved.

If you're in college, I'd encourage you to join faith-based organizations, where you're able to meet like-minded people who are also growing in their faith journey. Church also fits into this category, and a small group is always a great place to meet potential besties.

I cannot even describe how beautiful a Godly friendship is. No matter how messy you are, no matter how much you don't have your life together, no matter how racoon-ish you look with tears of mascara running down your face, a Godly friendship will point you to truth. It is a space that supports honesty, faith, authenticity - and then wraps it up with a bow of encouragement.

How To Make The First Step

When you decide what to get involved in, make sure you get your butt through the door of their building, even if it means going alone. This means church, a club, or even a bible study you've heard of.

There were plenty of times when I needed to suck it up and say tiny prayers as I walked into rooms alone. It was scary, even terrifying, but it all paid off in the end. Not everything that's worth doing is going to be fun, but the upside is worth the initial discomfort.

Finding a community requires putting yourself out there, even if it means first, second and maybe third tries.

You might've gotten shut down at church when you complimented Sally's shoes. But you can't let that destroy your hope for any future good friends. It's a good thing that there are nicer, cooler people than Sally out there - who would love to have a friend like you and are yearning for meaningful friendships.

I'll say it again: to have a friend you need to be a friend. Keep that in mind as you step into these meetings, that being a friend is more important than having a bunch of people swarm around you and tell you how amazing you are.

Shifting your focus off yourself and onto loving the people around you, even if you don't know them super well, will make the process a whole lot easier and comfortable.

If you don't know where to start, smile. Not a creepy smile, but a friendly-I'd-like-to-meet-you kind of smile. No one is a fan of a resting bitch face (RBF), and if you struggle with this default, try your best to resist.

And if you don't know what to say, ask a question. Ask other people what brought them to that meeting. Ask where they are from, and how their week is going, what brought them there. If making new friends is difficult for you, ask God to provide you with words and confidence to talk to people. People love to talk about themselves, so asking questions will always make for a good conversation.

After meeting someone, ask if they want to grab coffee. I know, I know, maybe you think that's pushy. And maybe you fear that you'll get rejected. But the truth is, everyone wants to be invited to something. It feels good to be wanted.

Our Steps Of Faith Matter

I remember mustering up the courage to go to a faith-based fitness class someone had referred me to. When I left the workout, I saw this girl walk home in the same direction. Her name was Carrie, and I quickly found out that our dorms were right next to each other. So after these weekly fitness classes, Carrie and I would regularly walk home together.

With each week, our friendship grew, and many tears and laughs were shared. She is now one of my best friends.

After meeting and hanging out with Carrie, she invited me to a bible study. I took Carrie's word for it and went to something called Huddle, where a bunch of women all met up at an upperclassman's house and talked about life.

One day, a new girl showed up. Emily had a ball cap on and she barely said a word. She came alone, so maybe that was why she was so quiet.

We didn't say much to each other, but with each small group meeting, our friendship grew more and more. Whether that was through breaking down the walls of the polished images we held, or through laughing until we cried at the ironies of college, our friendship blossomed into the best-friendship we have today.

All because of one step of faith.

If I had never mustered up the courage to go to the fitness class solo, I wouldn't have met Carrie. And if it weren't for Carrie, I wouldn't have met Emily. Each of these friendships started with a small act of faith, the belief that something better was out there.

Good things take time.

If a best-friendship happens in 2 weeks, that's a friendship built on a shaky foundation. True friendships take months of coffee dates, being vulnerable (ugly cry vulnerable), and laughing about awkward moments of the day.

But at the beginning of my venture, I hadn't quite figured this out. I was caught off guard when I didn't see immediate results from joining these clubs and bible studies.

I was hurt every time I turned to social media and saw that everyone else had found their people (or so it seemed). I felt a pang of jealousy every time I saw a big group walking to the dining hall, and I was heading off to my quiet dorm room to eat my sandwich alone.

I think sometimes God doesn't give us things to put on pedestals. I once heard an analogy that describes idols as stilts to prop up a house. If we are the house, we use different stilts to give us security. Eventually, God takes away each stilt one by one, so we can only rely on him.

God didn't forget about my hurt in high school. He heard my prayers about wanting community, and he had plans to give me that.

But he let me wait for it. And in the waiting, in the process of not getting what I wanted, I grew. I learned how to be content on my own and to put my identity in him before putting my worth in a group.

If I had looked in the future, I wouldn't have worried at all. If we always knew what the future held, there would be no point in having faith. In trusting a God who has our best interest in mind.

Now, two years after my first year in college, I am enjoying the blessings of a wonderful community. Of women who point each other to Jesus. Of women who mourn over the Bachelor. We cry together, pray together, hysterically laugh together.

I found the community I so hoped for in high school. And though a friend group didn't happen immediately, the Lord rewarded these steps of faith.

Love the season you're in

Your fun, uplifting, Jesus-loving friend group may not come immediately. But sometimes, the best ministry is loving the people right in front of us.

If it's one friend to confide in while you're looking for a Christian community, invest in that friendship. If you are blessed with a mentor, cherish that time together. Sometimes we have to be grateful for the small before God can entrust us with the big.

As someone who loves people, I've had trouble thinking that I need others around me to feel joy. And though friends are a wonderful gift, you don't need them to walk with confidence. True joy can be found no matter what the circumstances are.

There will always be something we don't have. The key is thanking God for what we do have, and living in the abundance of what we've been given.

Sometimes we think if we could only (fill in the blank), then we would be happy. But we don't need external things to be happy. There's so much goodness in loving the season God's put us in.

If you've been blessed with friends, love those friends well. But if you've done your part in finding them, and they still aren't there, it might mean God is calling you to walk in sweet intimacy with Him. He can be the best friend in the most lonely places.

If the time calls for you to be alone, you can grow closer to the Lord and enjoy the peace that comes with solitude. If the time calls for you to spend time with your bajillion friends, you can cultivate the wonderful gift of friendship and point them to Jesus.

I say this for the Friday nights when you are by yourself and don't have any plans. I say this for the nights when you have an endless number of options of what to do.

1 Corinthians 7:17 says, "And don't be wishing you were someplace else or with someone else. Where you are right now is God's place for you. Live and obey and love and believe right there." (1 Corinthians 7:17 MSG)

Where you are right now is no mistake. No matter the circumstance, you can thrive – and that's a promise.

Application

This week, try to get out of your comfort zone and take one step towards finding community. So whether that's getting plugged into church volunteering, joining a bible study, or asking another Christian to get coffee with you. One act of putting yourself out there can go a long way. You never know what amazing people are waiting on the other side of a bold step of faith.

A JOURNEY OF A LIFETIME

As we reach the end of this book, I want to congratulate you for taking a bold step in your faith journey. It's an honor that I get to walk alongside you in this journey of getting closer to the greatest relationship you could ever experience, to the best love out there.

I am more than excited for you to dig deeper into your faith. You might want to learn everything in the entire world in these next couple of months, and I totally get that. I was certainly the same way.

But I will tell you that getting closer to Jesus is going to take a lifetime. A lifetime of him molding you. And you'll be learning more and more about who he is in the meantime.

I am now 5 years after the day I googled Jesus, and I will tell you that I am still learning something new about God's character with each season I'm in. In the past few years, he's taken me through heartache, loss, grief, and insecurity. He's also shown me what true serenity looks like - joy, peace, and security as a child of God.

And the crazy thing is I'm only 21. I am still going to go through a million more things in my life, wherein each season God is the one holding my hand and teaching me more about who he is, and that I can trust him with every step I take.

This life with Jesus is a marathon, not a sprint. It's a journey that takes a lifetime, the most exciting roller coaster you could ever get a ticket for. God will show you more and more of who he is every day, and all he asks of you is to be open to the process.

And let me just tell you, not only will you see more of God's character, but you also will start to not recognize yourself. Believe it or not, the person you are now is not going to be familiar to you in the next couple of years. With each season you're in, each valley or mountaintop you climb, he will mold you more into the likeness of his character.

I'm reminded of what one friend told me the other day. I was talking about how the season I'm in has really changed me. And she said this - I don't think you've changed. I think you are just becoming more of the person that God destined you to be.

And the beautiful thing is we don't mold ourselves. Just like I tried to do on my own, I could not change myself to please those around me. He had literally knit me together before I was born, which he says in Psalm 139, "For you created my inmost being; you knit me together in my mother's womb."

When we open our hearts up to Him, He does the rest of the work. He does the work of changing you from the inside out, of giving you the fruits of the Spirit, of giving you forgiveness, kindness, goodness - and even self-control when you want to check Instagram 30 times a day. Okay, He will give you much more self-control than this, but this is a good start.

I am so honored that I could be there for you on this journey. You may be a beginner, but the Lord has so many incredible plans for you. I can't wait for him to take you to places you'd never thought you'd go, to new heights you'd never think you'd make it to.

He will walk you through rough, dark valleys - and he might be your only true friend at some points. But he will never leave you, no matter if you're at your peak, or if you are at rock bottom. After you accept him, he ain't going *anywhere*. You have a one-way ticket to a best friend for life.

Welcome to this new journey, my friend. May the Lord be ever so present in your life, guiding you and teaching you more about this wonderful thing called life. May the Lord be ever so present with you in every season - whether it be a dark valley or a beautiful mountaintop. May He always light the path for you in this thing called life - so no matter how dark it gets, the flashlight still shines.

For more, follow along online!
Instagram: @thehoneyscoop
www.thehoneyscoop.com

ABOUT THE AUTHOR

Ashley Hetherington is a lifestyle blogger who created *The Honey Scoop*, a platform designed to add a sweet scoop of encouragement to your day. She has a passion for writing life-giving words to others and telling stories that make people think. Ashley is a junior at Miami University majoring in Journalism, and she enjoys reading books, asking deep questions, and scrolling the shoes on the Nordstrom's website. She hopes to lead you towards a life of fullness and wonder.

ENDNOTES & REFERENCES

How I Ended Up Googling Jesus

1. Ralph Waldo Emerson. *Self Reliance.*
   http://www.rwe.org/complete-works/ii---essays-i/ii-self-reliance,
   Accessed 13 November 2019.
2. Warren, Rick. *The Purpose Driven Life.* Zondervan, 2013.

How Do I Talk To God?
1. "Series Premiere" *This Is Us.* NBC. 20 Sept. 2016. Television.

Church 101
1. The Head And The Heart. *The Head And The Heart.* Sub Pop, 2010.
2. Furtick, Steven, pastor. *Elevation With Steven Furtick, iTunes* app, 2013.
3. Transformation Church. *Transformation Church, iTunes* app, 2016.
4. Crossroads Church. https://media.crossroads.net/series/

How To Spend Your Mornings
1. Jim Branch. *The Blue Book: A Devotional Guide for Every Season of Your Life.* CreateSpace Independent Publishing Platform, 2016.
2. First 5. *Proverbs 31 Ministry,* 2019. Version 2.9.13. *Apple App Store.* https://itunes.apple.com/us/app/first-5/id997457664?mt=8.
3. Sarah Young. *Jesus Calling: Enjoying Peace In His Presence.* Thomas Nelson, 2004.
4. Love God Greatly. *Love God Greatly, Inc,* 2019. Version 4.12.5. *Apple App Store.* https://itunes.apple.com/us/app/love-god-greatly/id1112318135?mt=8.

I Have A Bible, But What Do I Do With It?

1. CSB Bibles by Holman, Raechel Myers, Amanda Bible Williams. *CSB She Reads Truth Bible Hardcover.* B&H Publishing Group, 2017.
2. Hosanna Revival. *HOSANNA REVIVAL BIBLE.* . https://hosannarevival.com/collections/beautiful-bibles/products/hosanna-bible-lisbon-theme.
3. Zondervan. *NIV, Journal the Word Bible, Leathersoft, Brown/Blue, Red Letter Edition, Comfort Print: Reflect, Take Notes, or Create Art Next to Your Favorite Verses.* Zondervan, 2018.
4. Verses - Bible Memory. *Verses, Ltd. Co,* Mar 13, 2019. Version 5.3.3. https://itunes.apple.com/us/app/verses-bible-memory/id939461663?mt=8.
5. "The Bible Project." YouTube. YouTube, n.d. Web. 22 March 2019.
6. She Reads Truth. *She Reads Truth,* Feb 9, 2019. Version 3.2.1. *Apple App Store.* https://penandthepad.com/cite-youtube-mla-format-6161761.html.
7. Thesauras.com. https://www.thesaurus.com/
8. Bible Study Tools. *Bible Dictionary.*
9. https://www.biblestudytools.com/dictionaries/.
10. John Piper. *Desiring God.* https://www.desiringgod.org/.
11. Bible. *Life.Church,* Mar 13, 2019. Version 8.9. *Apple App Store.* https://itunes.apple.com/us/app/bible/id282935706?mt=8.

Give Me A W For Worship

1. Hillsong Worship. https://hillsong.com/worship/.
2. Elevation Worship. https://elevationworship.com/.
3. Bethel Music. *You Make Me Brave.* +180 RECORDS, 2014.
4. Lauren Daigle. https://laurendaigle.com/.
5. Stephanie Gretzinger. "Out Of Hiding." *The Undoing,* 2014 Bethel Music. https://itunes.apple.com/us/album/the-undoing/910383995?app=itunes&ign-mpt=uo%3D4.
6. Michael W. Smith. "Surrounded (Fight My Battles)." *Moments.* Rocketown Records/The Fuel Music. https://www.youtube.com/watch?v=YBl84oZxnJ4.
7. UPPERROOM. "Worthy of it all (All of the glory)." https://www.urdallas.com/.

8. Jonathan David and Melissa Helser. "Beautiful Surrender." Bethel Music. https://bethelmusic.com/albums/beautiful-surrender/.
9. Cory Asbury. "Reckless Love." *Reckless Love*. Bethel Music. https://bethelmusic.com/chords-and-lyrics/reckless-love/.
10. Kings (MHM). "Come Thou Fount." *Asaph's Arrows*. BEC Recordings. https://itunes.apple.com/us/album/asaphs-arrows-ep/963247251.
11. Martin Luther King Jr, *From the estate of Dr. Martin Luther King, Jr.* https://www.goodreads.com/quotes/659576-and-when-you-discover-what-you-will-be-in-your.